GETTING IN SHAPE FOR
Skin & Scuba Diving

COMPANION TITLES FROM NEW CENTURY

The New Science of Skin and Scuba Diving

The New Science of Skin and Scuba Diving Workbook

First Aid for Boaters and Divers

Lifesaving and Marine Safety

GETTING IN SHAPE FOR
Skin & Scuba Diving

CURTIS MITCHELL

Association Press
NEW CENTURY PUBLISHERS, INC.

Printing Code
11   12   13   14   15   16

Library of Congress Cataloging in Publication Data

Mitchell, Curtis.
  Getting in shape for skin and scuba diving.

  Includes index.
  1. Scuba diving. 2. Physical education and
training. 3. Physical fitness. I. Title.
GV840.S78M56   797.2'3   81-11227
ISBN 0-8329-0114-8   AACR2

Contents

Preface   vii

Chapter 1
Welcome to Skin and Scuba Diving   1

Chapter 2
The New Science of Physical Fitness   8

Chapter 3
Start Where You Are   22

Chapter 4
Conditioning Drills to Improve Your Skills   38

Chapter 5
A Perfect Dive Every Time   53

Chapter 6
Oxygen, Carbon Dioxide, and the Human Body   60

Chapter 7
Diving Maladies   68

Chapter 8
Topside Hazards   85

Index   155

Preface

This book is intended to answer the question: What does a sport diver *need* to know to insure his or her safety and delight in the hobby?

I believe that a diver needs to know, in general, that most divers do not possess the physical reserves to survive many of the crises that occur underwater.

I believe that he needs to know the degree of his own fitness or lack of it, and to understand that reconditioning of a less-than-robust physique can be achieved swiftly and economically if the will to do so exists.

"Spot" improvements by means of isometric exercises are one option. Aerobic training for holistic fitness is another. And there is always self-conditioning through the ideal exercise, swimming.

But there is more to sport diving than being in good shape. I believe a diver needs to know about the space-age chain of instrumentation that enables a man or woman at the bottom of a lake to breathe fresh air whether dismantling a wreck or merely rubbernecking. To protect himself, he also needs to know about the new maladies that this booming sport has introduced into medical practice, thus to shield himself from the misinformation of others.

Finally, he needs to know that many of the ordinary injuries suffered during diving expeditions can be treated effectively by anyone with a suitable guidebook and a kit of first-aid supplies. Among the happy consequences of such treatment is a considerable saving through the elimination of fees for medicine and medical services. Nor should anyone deprecate the extra hours of diving time made possible by prompt attention to bugs and bruises.

Becoming fit for diving as a hobby is certainly to be praised, but the ultimate pay-off can be much more gratifying. Fitness is needed throughout life. Habits learned in a scuba school, if prolonged into later years, can pay a bonus of fitness, self-confidence, competence, and enduring friendship.

Few sports offer such satisfactions.

Few sportsmen can contemplate such a reward.

Curtis Mitchell

A Word of Caution to the Reader

The medical and physical procedures contained in the text of this book are accepted as common practice among swimmers and sport divers and are offered only as suggestions for use where no harmful effects to an individual might be expected to result. The author and publisher disclaim responsibility for any adverse effect resulting from the use of the information contained herein and strongly advise the reader to seek competent medical advice before undertaking any action that might produce a deleterious or otherwise undesirable result.

GETTING IN SHAPE FOR
Skin & Scuba Diving

1

Welcome to Skin and Scuba Diving

To don flippers, mask, and scuba gear is to join a unique fellowship of freedom-seeking spirits. Divers are bound together by the discovery of truths that land-bound mortals have not yet learned and by the camaraderie of the spectacular underwater kingdoms they have visited.

But there is one unpleasant problem. Too many free divers are thwarted in their quest for longer excursions and deeper penetration of their underwater paradise. Too many drop out. Too many are injured. Too many perish.

Why should this be?

No other recreational activity has expanded so fast. No sport is supported by such fine-honed technology. No human endeavor has brought participants such technicolored experiences amid such picturesque locales.

But something is amiss; and until recently, nobody was willing to talk about it—not that it was a secret. Now that the lid is off, talk has finally begun.

What everybody has been so reluctant to discuss is the physical unfitness of America's current crop of applicants for certification. At last, they are talking about the results of our automated way of life—call it the waterbed society—which have eroded the human spirit and diluted the will to excel.

"I get too many kids who can't stand the gaff and quit," a veteran instructor reports.

"They come in my shop and order diving gear like it's going out of style. God knows where they get the money. Two months later they're worrying me to death by forgetting to bring a spare light on a cave dive," says another.

"It's these young couples that I worry about," a Florida resort owner complained. They've been big in college athletics maybe, but when they come here after having a baby or two, they're overweight and undermuscled. Just putting on their gear, they get a heart rate of a hundred and thirty. That's scary!"

At a recent international convention of YMCA skin and scuba activists, physical fitness for diving was one of the topics most hotly debated. Associations of professional instructors are equally concerned, and so are dive-shop owners.

At stake for professionals in the field is their livelihood. For amateurs, their risks run from injury to loss of their lives.

Aren't we as fit as we need to be? Astronaut Wally Shirra is reported as saying, "If you can breathe, you can dive." Think twice before you accept that at face value. Shirra was the recipient of a million dollars worth of physical conditioning fitting him to ride a space capsule. When he spoke, he was one of America's most perfectly conditioned individuals.

To be sure, the jogging boom is in full cry on every city street, in magazines and books, in marathons taking place from Boston to Hawaii. Who needs more fitness? Well, the fact is that serious joggers are fit, have trained themselves by running up to 100 miles each week. If a jogger wants to become a diver, hooray. He's got the heart and legs for it. But turn the situation around. What if a diver wants to become a jogger, what's he got?

Let's face it! Most divers are unfit for jogging and they don't even know it. And if they are unfit for jogging, they've got no business going underwater. That's what the talking is all about. That's what leading divers are saying.

"Physical coordination and stamina are not built up by an hour's workout once a week," says John Sweeney, author and diver. "Swimming under water, especially with spear, camera, or collecting apparatus, requires the finest coordination of mind and body."

Tom Mount and Akim J. Ikehara, diving officers of Miami University's School of Marine and Atmospheric Science, assert,

"It can be truthfully said that the physically unfit person is unfit for diving. Man must be physically fit and must develop physical skills to be efficient in the water."

Paul J. Tzimoulis, editor and publisher of *Skin Diver* magazine, writes, "A good diver keeps himself in basically good physical condition so that he can enjoy his dives and avoid panic situations."

Joe Strykowski, national chairman of the YMCA Underwater Program, writes, "The average sport diver, relying exclusively on his participation in diving activities for a high level of physical fitness, does not develop—nor maintain—the high level of conditioning he needs. It is clear that the diving undertaken by the average sport diver is not sufficient in itself."

Speaking to YMCA diving instructors at the YMCA Underwater Activities Center in Key West, Strykowski added, "Technology has become a substitute for the diver's own senses and an awareness of the body's inner signals. Each new piece of equipment makes us less and less reliant on ourselves. Our technological 'overkill' has not made us better divers. Rather, it has robbed us of our instinctive need to develop our physical skills and senses."

A diving manual recently summed it up like this: "Swimming under water is one of the most stressful exercises a man can do. Even carrying your scuba tank and weight belt on land is demanding of your strength and endurance. Obviously, you should be in good physical condition, for sooner or later you will find yourself in a situation which demands physical prowess."

Physical prowess or physical fitness: What is it and what does it offer a diver? Perhaps the best definition is the one that gives this four-fold answer.

First, it is more than the absence of disease.

Second, it is having the strength and endurance to accomplish one's daily tasks.

Third, it provides energy for the enjoyment of a program of vigorous recreation and sport as well as participation in family and community projects.

Fourth, it provides the inner strength that enables one to cope with whatever unexpected crises may occur.

Maybe what fooled everybody is the fact that divers are also swimmers. And swimming is great exercise. Everyone says so. And maybe it is the best, if one swims. But how many swimmers really swim? Most of them learned in backyard pools, above-the-ground tanks, or at public beaches with parasols and hamburger stands. What one does as a child one does as an adult. Look around at any aquatic center and note the activity. You will see plenty of splashing, chatting, diving, sunning, horsing around and frisbee throwing, but precious little flat-out swimming.

Sure, swimming is the greatest exercise around, but the guys and gals who do it aren't sitting around building sand castles. They are swimming laps.

What's to be done?

First, project yourself into the situation. Scuba diving is not like backpacking and camping. In those activities, you can pick up an outfit—from togs to tents—from L. L. Bean and be hiking in the Sierras tomorrow. Nor is it like skiing, which allows you to step into your boots at dawn, no instructor present, and be schussing down a slope by mid-morning.

Scuba diving is more like learning to fly an airplane. Nobody takes off without an instructor. Nobody flies alone until he has passed mental and physical examinations. A flyer *knows* before he *goes*. So should a scuba diver.

Believe the old hands of scuba diving when you hear them say that the sport does not provide enough exercise to create fitness. If you understand and accept this fact, you may live to a ripe old age. If you reject it, you will be joining all those others who ride over fairways in their golf carts or spend their nights rolling balls down bowling alleys convinced that their sport is contributing to their health. Physiologists have proved that both sports are enjoyable and that they maintain some muscle tone and body flexibility, but as fitness builders they are flops.

What builds fitness, research tells us, is activity that makes the body *sweat*. What makes a body sweat is activity that demands of the muscles of both body and heart a little more exertion than is their habit.

What builds fitness is the repetition of muscular contractions for periods varying from ten to thirty consecutive minutes each and every day—or at least four days every week.

The fitness a diver needs will not be provided by such stand-around games as baseball, volleyball, or tennis doubles. A diver needs the head-to-head confrontation provided by tennis singles, badminton, racquetball, or lacrosse. Other winners are jogging, rowing, biking, jumping rope, swimming, basketball, mountain climbing, cross-country skiing, and even long-distance walking.

Second, know yourself. Are you the physical person you can and ought to be? Do you know why skin tightens with apprehension or your heart pounds when you despair? Chapter 2 will provide some clues. Do you know the toughness of your heart? Would a bench test put it in the poor, medium, or excellent category? There are more clues in Chapter 3. Most important, do you know how to *change* your innermost muscle fibers, nerve filaments, and the flowing currents of blood and plasma that feed your cells so that each contributes to the vigor and self-confidence for which your body was designed? Some of these secrets are revealed in Chapter 4.

Finally, do you know that personal dedication and commitment— it used to be called will power—are even more important to a diver than the world's finest, space-age regulator?

Are you willing to make such a commitment?

If you are, you can look for a double blessing. First, improved fitness will multiply your enjoyment of every dive.

Second, you will come to understand that fitness lasts a lifetime. As the months become years, you will discover a new kind of music in your body.

Shall we look briefly at a partial list of the benefits of fitness? A host of researchers and their scientific publications support every claim.

Fitness slows the decline of muscular strength that begins in most persons at the age of thirty. Vigorous exercise postpones physical decay.

The heart learns to increase its pumping capacity while using fewer strokes. Heart muscle rests between strokes. The fewer strokes per minute, the longer the rest periods between beats. A rested heart conserves stamina, storing it away for emergency.

The diaphragm and the leg muscles that help the heart move blood through the body become stronger and less likely to cramp or tire.

The threat of heart attack is reduced because arteries that become blocked with atherosclerosis are able to build new blood pathways (collateral circulation) under the stimulus of vigorous activity. The formation of atherosclerosis in the arteries is discouraged and sometimes reversed.

The accumulation of unsightly fat deposits is controlled.

Nerves are soothed and anxiety is ameliorated.

The body that once tired becomes rugged and sturdy, and when it occasionally grows weary it recovers overnight.

Reflecting the body, the mind functions crisply and decisively.

The senses purge themselves of impurities and deliver vivid stimuli to the brain, thus reshaping and recoloring one's outlook.

Reaction time decreases significantly so that the limbs respond instantaneously as messages from motor neurons reach the brain where they are processed and answered during the wink of an eye. Skills are enhanced beyond compare.

Stress becomes your ally. Some stress is needed if the body is to become stronger. Moderate stresses countered by moderate increments of planned activity help muscles to adapt.

Aggression, envy, resentment, and jealousy are modified—and sometimes eliminated forever. Exercise drains off one's anger and pacifies the spirit. Psychosomatic disorders are rare in fit persons.

The fit person is served by battalions of red blood cells, and by extra squadrons of white cells to guard one's tissues against invasions of infection.

Finally, there is the miracle of better breathing. Conditioning programs dramatically change the lungs and the way they function. Their capacity increases. They learn to relax and return quickly to a normal breathing speed despite vigorous stimulation. They begin to transfer more oxygen per heartbeat so that each enables the body to do more work—an invaluable gift to divers active in deep water. In short, one breathes more slowly and deeply, exactly as divemasters propose.

Is this enough?

Ask your body. Let it whisper to your brainstem about the pains it feels, the pleasures it enjoys. If your mind says there's no time for exercise, remind it that injury and illness lurk at the edge of darkness waiting to bushwhack a tiring muscle, an overstressed bone, or a scratchy throat. If they strike, they will take as much of your time as they want. Only you can forestall them. On your next dive, listen to your body.

All great divers have done so, starting with Cousteau, who—working with an associate—persevered until he perfected his Aqualung. So have our great undersea photographers and the scientists who go to the seabed to study. They have learned that diving is more scientific than athletic, and they have followed their separate fitness routines in order to reinforce their bodies.

Once upon a time, it was perhaps enough to be a "natural-born" athlete. Today, one has to work at it. Quarterback Roger Staubach, whose fruitful career ended in 1980, spent more hours in Dr. Kenneth Cooper's Aerobics Fitness Center in Dallas than he did playing football. All-American players from many sports are regular off-season visitors to the conditioning machines of the Nautilus Corporation in Lake Helen, Florida.

In the business world, the top executives of three thousand corporations have begun to take part in programmed exercises because they realize that weekend sports such as golf and tennis are not enough.

Fortunately, it is never too late.

If you would like to increase the pleasures of your diving, you can join this movement.

These next chapters can be your guide.

2

The New Science of Physical Fitness

Divers who have discovered the delights of loitering beside a coral head in sixty feet of water know the pleasure of experiencing a new world. Its sights are unprecedented and colorful beyond anything known topside. Its cool lavings encase the human body with resilient support. No other sensation on earth is like it.

This chapter introduces the sport diver to another world that is equally salubrious. Few of us ever get to know this world and its wonders, but its voices are with us from birth, through adolescence, and into our maturity. It is the inner world of our bodies. Here are marvels galore, if only we come to know them through participation in the art and science of physical fitness.

De La Mettre calls the body "a machine that winds its own springs."

But how does it wind its own springs? Rousseau asked for strength. "A weak body weakens the mind," he said. When the springs are wound, what then? Strength and stamina are two rewards of physical fitness that every diver needs. To borrow from Mark Twain, "the difference between the fit person and the unfit is the difference between lightning and the lightning bug."

The body is a vast republic of cells—a democracy in which every cell is a citizen. Today, we are discovering that these good citizens within us rejoice and develop stamina only in movement and vigorous activity.

Why do we tire? At one time, scientists who studied the question declared that life's stresses have become too much for our citizenry of cells. Today, researchers are discovering new truths; namely, that life has always been stressful and difficult. Our trouble is that our bodies have become inadequate, our blood and bones more delicate than those of our forebears, our muscles weaker, and our organs more vulnerable.

Yet science is also telling us that the process is reversible. Whether one dives for recreation or jogs for relaxation, one is returning to a process that commenced in the mists of prehistory. The first men on earth were swimmers and fishermen. They used their limbs to activate their internal organs and to swell their muscle fibers as they fought or fled before the hobgoblins of their era.

This book is an effort to provide a better understanding of the physiological miracle called man. It is my hope that a more complete comprehension of what we humans once were and have now become will release many from the slavery of unfitness. Standing in the way of this release are ignorance about the latent powers of the body and the habitual slothfulness of a generation conditioned to instant cookery, push-button locomotion, and narcotic-induced sleep.

KNOW YOUR SKIN

The skin—outer husk or covering of the body—comprises two main layers. The outer layer is composed of flat, horny cells that fit about the body like elastic armor. The inner layer is a garden of nerve endings, capillaries, hair follicles, and sweat cells.

Your skin never sleeps. Its seamless shield fends off attacks by noxious bacteria and viruses. Its envelopment prevents the leakage of body fluids. More than that, its minute perforations (pores) permit the regulation of the body's temperature (through the evaporation of sweat and the elimination of wastes). Finally, it holds a network of computerized sensing devices that send an endless stream of data about heat, cold, pain, pressure, and touch to the brain.

In special areas, the skin produces a hairy crop growing from follicles which can contract under the stimulus of fear to lift the hairs of the head until they "stand on end." If cold breezes blow, they can erect futile goose bumps (the remnants of inherited hair glands) that might have kept a caveman warm but perform no service whatever today.

Your skin is your facade, often announcing your occupation or disposition. Amazingly, it is never the same on two successive days, for it is involved in an endless process of erosion. At its point of contact with the sun, wind, or aerial pollutants, its outermost cells dry up like shingles on a roof, curling at the edges, browning with liverish spots, and finally perishing. Daily, they expire and drift away by the millions. Concurrently, a continuous process of body magic replaces them, and our innards remain safe from invasion for a few more hours. (See sunburn)

KNOW YOUR BLOOD

Blood, or some of its elements, penetrates every fragment of tissue within your skin. The tissues it fails to penetrate (like hair and fingernails) are actually dead but renewed constantly from living roots. On the average, a man possesses five or six quarts of this salt-tinctured solution; a woman, one quart less. Its health depends on its warmth, its acidity, and a floating population of platelets and corpuscles, white and red, that are said to number from twenty-five thousand to thirty thousand *billion* cells.

Legend tells us that blood possesses a mystical power. Even kings subscribed to the notion, for history relates that King Louis XI of France sought relief from a painful malady by drinking the blood of several infants. His effort failed. And a Roman pope, infirm and afraid, quaffed the blood of willing young acolytes, hoping to extend his years. He died.

Blood is red because its red cells or corpuscles carry a smidgin of iron in the hemoglobin that possesses a magical affinity with oxygen and with carbon dioxide. This affinity induces the transfer within the lungs (from inhaled air) of oxygen into the blood stream and simultaneously the countertransfer of carbon dioxide into air that will be exhaled.

A red cell lives only three or four months. Racing through the rivers within your body, it bumps through "white water" stretches and runs aground on calcified shoals, tearing its delicate hide and often splitting into fragments. The body eliminates this debris and replaces it with new cells at dizzying speed. Scientists tell us that red cells are born in the marrow of our bones at the rate of ten million per second. That production is needed, they say, to match the death rate of worn-out cells.

White cells are called leucocytes, and a body that runs short of them will not long remain alive. White cells number only about fifty million. Their role is to cleanse the blood and tissues. Germs, microbes, bacteria, and viruses are their enemies. Patrolling their arterial turf, or stationed in fleshy fortresses, they possess a mysterious communications system that alerts them like a bugle call and sends them into kamikazi conflict. They expect no mercy, they extend no mercy. Kill or be killed is their battle cry.

After death, and they perish by the millions, they are quarantined from healthy tissue by an encircling host of triumphant leucocytes. Their cemetery can be what we sometimes call a boil. Their jellied corpses are what we call pus.

Equally important components of the blood are boat-shaped wisps of protein called platelets. Slippery as wet soap, they glide endlessly through the body's passages, part of a floating Maginot Line waiting only to be assembled in the face of an enemy. They are so tiny that a quarter of a million would scarcely cover the head of a pin. Alongside them, but moving independently until needed, are wispy threads of protein called fibrinogen. At impact, at a broaching of the defensive skin that protects your body, they thrust themselves into the breach and automatically arrange themselves in sticky webs that, like a fisherman's minnow net, catch passing platelets and shape them into the miraculous defensive structures we call scabs.

A blood count of platelets is one of the most useful devices for estimating health. Indeed, a variation of it is said to be responsible for winning an Olympic swimming meet. A coach's responsibility includes bringing athletes to their contests at their peak. Too much training can result in staleness. Several years ago, an Australian swimming coach brooded on this matter. He knew that white cells began to multiply at the invasion of germs or at too much stress. So he began to make a weekly count of his swimmer's platelets. A normal allotment was five to ten million cells per cubic millimeter. When any swimmer's count rose above that figure—or when a swimmer grew bored and had an "I don't care" attitude—he was ordered to rest for a couple of days. And his white corpuscle count dropped.

It was a great discovery. That year, every Australian came to his event "riding the racer's edge." And they swept the Olympics.

Blood travels fast. It circles through the body at about two minutes per circuit. If it stops for any reason, the brain—which uses almost one-half of the total supply—becomes a useless blob within four to six minutes.

The body's arteries (out-going vessels) and veins (incoming vessels) range from tubes as thick as a man's thumb to filaments as fine as baby hair, called capillaries, that permeate tissue everywhere, trickling food and oxygen constantly into thirsty tissues. The bloodstream collects its cargo of oxygen in the lungs and its cargo of processed nutrients in the intestines.

Within the lungs, tired blood dumps its refuse and scoops up fresh oxygen like a locomotive rolling along a railway watering trough. Within seconds, work-weary corpuscles are revitalized and moved through the heart to serve the unending needs of brain and brawn.

KNOW YOUR BONES

You have a couple of hundred bones within your body, and almost all of them are workers, each harnessed to another worker.

Their function, most of us believe, is to support their wrapping of flesh. That is only the beginning. Bones are alive—breathing, living, and dying each day of your existence.

Their outside layers are as hard as rock. Some of them are stronger than oaken beams. Pound for pound, they are stronger than steel. Their insides are factories, narrow tunnels filled with a mush of fantastic tissue that produces ten million blood cells per second.

Some bones are semisoft, like the vertebrae of the spine. Solid enough to sustain the three curves of the backbone, they are also elastic enough to give way without shattering when the body jackknifes in a fall. Because of this quality, truly broken backs are rare, but compressed vertebrae (compression fractures) are not.

Within the skeleton, the flow of blood is as continuous and as vital as its flow through muscles. In addition to creating corpuscles and feeding them into the bloodstream, bones also harbor minerals that are dispensed from hidden depositories at the body's demand.

Just as the skin erodes and replaces itself, so do bones. The process is too gradual to observe, but it progresses inexorably. Over each seven-year period of life, every bone in the body has been renewed. This renewal is quickest and strongest, physiologists declare, when the body is regularly used with vigor.

Bones break, of course, but they heal with remarkable speed. And so perfectly are they endowed with nerves and served with nutrients that when the healing is over no trace of scarring remains. Nor any weakness either. The broken leg that is reset properly, it's said, is stronger than its mate.

KNOW YOUR NERVES

We've got nerves on and under our skin, laced into our muscles, and infused into our bones. We sit on them, taste with them, and mate with them.

Two hundred thousand receptors tell us if we're too hot or too cold. Three thousand adorn our tongue. One hundred thousand serve each ear. And over one hundred million enable us to see in living color.

Nerves are not isolated star-points in the universe of our bodies. They communicate with each other. In the last half-dozen years, neurologists have discovered more nerve circuits than had been known since the beginning of time.

All told, our nerves may have about ten trillion connections, each neuron able to communicate with a million others. It's enough to make Ma Bell green with envy. Despite their numbers, not one man in a million has ever seen a nerve. That experience is limited to those at the dissecting table in a human performance lab.

So let's draw a picture of an average, everyday grassroots nerve. Well, it's a wavy line on a piece of paper—if you're using a pencil—that can be as short as a baby's toe as long as a yardstick. Give one end of the line (the axon) a bewhiskered head (neuron) and the other end a tapered tail. Duplicate it until your count holds so many zeros it looks like a spaced-out caterpillar. That's approximately your body's nerve supply. If all those nerves were placed end to end, they would reach to the moon and back. You've got one billion neurons. They touch everything within the skin, they work day and night, just as long as your movements provide them with the nourishment they draw from your blood.

Each neuron is akin to a storage battery that constantly recharges itself. Each axon has branches, and each of these branches has other branches, which turn into twigs that connect with other twigs leading to muscle bundles and blood vessels. So complicated is this network that some researchers have devoted their lives to understanding the nervous system of a single frog.

What concerns us here is the tiny jolt of electricity with which an axon can stimulate its muscular attachment to take some action. This change originates in the polywog head of the nerve cell and flows at a speed up to three hundred miles per hour. It fires like a machine gun in graduated bursts from slow to rapid. Athletes have been known to condition themselves to raise their rapid fire level to hundreds of jolts per minute. When that happens, their muscles harden with massive contractions, which produce world records.

Each neuron head wears a set of cat's whiskers called dendrites. In the dampness of its skin-roofed universe, a dendrite picks up faint vibes. The signal comes from the tail of an adjacent axon. The dendrite's pores open to emit a chemical that floods the intervening space, intensifying the signal, conducting it to the neuronhead—turning on its battery, as it were, like throwing a switch in a powerhouse. The juice flows along the transmission line to another powerhouse, where the process is repeated. We've described the operation of a trio of cells. You are inhabited by a billion, each one sparking invisibly, filling your mind with memories, impulses, regrets, ambition, joy, and pain.

Signals run both ways—to the brain and from the brain. A simple and much-used example is that of the unwary finger that touches a hot stove. A pain receptor (you've got two hundred thousand of them) picks up the menacing heat and originates an emergency message. Nerve conduction routes it to your brain. Inside your skull (with its own one-billion neurons) a complicated but almost instantaneous transaction takes place. Your experiences are stored there in display charts imbedded in patterns of neurons. With millions of interconnections, an action center selects the appropriate action, and dispatches an order over a hot-line of axons running back to the sizzling finger. The order says, "Jerk your finger away, dope!" It happens in 1/200 of the time it takes to blink an eye.

We live in the age of the computer. We respect and admire computers as marvels of technology. But the computer has not yet been assembled that can hold a candle to man's brain. The intricacies of the human brain are hard to grasp, but let's try. The evolution of the brain began with a knobby brain stem and a spinal cord of nerve cells woven together like jungle vines. All animals had the same equipment, developed to manage an unquenchable drive for self-preservation, and to provide coordination for feeding, walking, running, fighting, and mating.

As time marched ahead, the knobby stem expanded into what is called a cortex. For the first time, primitive man learned to classify his experiences as either painful or pleasurable. It was an important distinction. It enabled him to distinguish friend from foe. It gave him the mental equipment to outwit wild beasts, tidal waves, and hairy migrants who invaded his territory.

Much more recently, a third development increased man's

worth and worries. An unprecedented assortment of brain cells sprouted from his cortex to push against the interior of his slanting forehead. As the cranial bones moved forward and upward to become lofty brows, the space behind them filled with what are now called prefrontal lobes. These are colonies of nerve cells with unique and special abilities. Here dwell the qualities we call imagination, wisdom, conscience, value, and guilt.

But to return to the muscle, what is the power that produces a knock-out blow? Scientists who have counted the bursts of neural electricity that move a muscle say that the swift, all-out kick of a mule's hind-leg is the result of a burst so tightly spaced that individual impulses seem to merge into one explosion. The leisurely sweep of a pair of swim fins, on the other hand, is energized by a relaxed rat-a-tat-tat.

What initiates muscle power? It comes from the will. What energizes the will? Its origin is in a person's experience. What is experience? It is conditioning (some call it training) that provides a background of painful or pleasurable events that trace deep patterns among his brain's neurons so that the muscular response is appropriate and effective.

Nerves are at work everywhere. Do you feel cold? Nerves read the temperature, expand the capillaries that carry warm blood to the skin, and direct the warming flow into your peripheral circulation. If you feel hot, other nerves open sweat glands and release a salty liquid that spreads along the skin, evaporating to cool it. When you execute a dive, nerves tell you which end is up. Some nerves resist training, responding to tense situations by unruly reactions that we call "butterflies in the stomach." Some nerves accept training. In a proficient diver, as in a soldier, they learn their duty and perform it better and better with experience. We say such a diver has "nerves of steel."

I refer again to Dr. Arthur Steinhouse, one of America's greatest physiologists, for a picture of the patterns laid down among the body's power lines. He told his students to imagine nerve impulses burning their trails through the body at an average speed of 150 miles per hour. He compared their axons to firecracker wicks that connected ultimately with the brain. Some wicks run like superhighways while others meander like the paths of wandering cattle.

The development of a human's experiences is best imagined perhaps by picturing a town at dawn. Snow has fallen during the night. Not a tire track or footprint marks the snowy covering. But presently cars and trucks enter the scene. The first car leaves a crusted trail through the town. The tracks of the second car cross those of the first, and those of the third vehicle cross both earlier arrivals, enlarging the pattern. If those vehicles had been nerve impulses, each crossing would have formed a permanent connection. In time, the fourth and fifth vehicles and the tenth and twentieth would create ruts. Now imagine those ruts to be nerve axons in the brain. And imagine the nerve impulses to be tiny mice coming down that country road into town. As they hit the first rut, some of them turn off to explore it while others scamper ahead. As they proceed, they spill into other ruts, veering again and again into other ruts. Some make a loop and return to the original pathway. Others run into dead ends. These ruts can be compared to memory. When they become so deep that we follow them automatically, they become habits. Some ruts lead us to commendable activities. Some lead to antisocial escapades.

Thus, blood and bone and muscle and nerves combine to build a human being capable both of astonishing achievements and of gratifying pleasures. This essay is meant to provide an understanding of the powerful and frequently neglected systems that back up every physical performance.

Blood and bone and flesh and nerves *must* work together if the goal of safety is to be reached and the activity is to endure. The key to survival is movement. Activity within the human husk is a prime consideration. Activity of the human body for as long as one lives is essential if the internal dynamism is to be maintained and the joys of youthfulness are to be realized year after year.

To that end, we suggest in Chapter 3 some methods of examining your own body and its potential, and of looking at yourself, perhaps as if through the eyes of great divers of the past.

KNOW YOUR CIRCULATION

We stand in awe of the beauty of the stars and the precision of their flight each night; but there are greater marvels within every human. One of these is the irrigation system that we call our circulation. Actually, it is a rushing river.

This river rises in a four-chambered marvel we call the heart. It is really a simple double-pump. Its left side drives blood through the body's blood-transport system of arteries and veins. Its right side drives blood through the body's blood-scrubbing apparatus that we call the lungs. The perfection of its operation is beyond belief.

The left side, which attends to the general circulation, has two chambers, one above the other. The upper chamber is called an atrium. The lower chamber is called a ventricle. The atrium collects fresh blood newly arrived from the lungs, then pumps it into the powerful lower chamber which closes on it like a giant fist, forcing it into a feeder line that we call the aorta.

Between contractions (beats) the heart rests. In contraction after contraction, it moves your entire blood supply, which may be five or six quarts, into the body through the aorta, thence through large arteries, then to smaller arteries, and into very small arteries called arterioles.

A word about those arteries. Each is a three-ply hose with a lining of pearl-slick tissue that expedites the delivery of blood. The outer layer is a thin sheet of muscle which, like all muscle, is permeated by its own blood supply (for nourishment) and by nerve twigs (for control). Directed by an automatic computer in the brain, arteries expand or contract, thus enlarging or reducing the blood flow and shifting it to wherever it is needed most. The arteries of fit people are soft and supple; those of unfit people are often clogged by cholesterol deposits. These deposits may eventually turn to calcium, hardening, and make life miserable with pain and dizziness. Doctors call this hardening of the arteries. Seemingly there is no remedy—except regular exercise three to five times each week.

Blood flows into the body's arterial tree like sap into an oak or elm, penetrating its dividing branches until it arrives ultimately at a special kind of blood vessel called a capillary. These number in the millions. Their porous walls are only one cell thick. Some are like hollow baby hair, with passageways so narrow that blood corpuscles must wiggle through one at a time.

Each red cell in the bloodstream carries a cargo of oxygen imprisoned in its hemoglobin. In the capillaries, oxygen is allowed to escape. It is immediately swallowed up by thirsty tissues, which are in the process of creating energy. Thus, the fires of metabolism keep burning.

A capillary is more than a nozzle at the end of a hose. Simultaneously, it is a drain pipe. Through its tissue-thin walls, a reverse flow takes place in which products created by the body's metabolic process feed into the bloodstream. Working muscle cells create a poisonous by-product called carbon dioxide that must be removed before it paralyzes. The hemoglobin in red blood cells attracts carbon dioxide much as a magnet attracts iron filings. Once it is pulled into the capillary, it is embraced by passing red cells and begins its journey to the lungs.

The route is similar to that followed by outward bound blood, but now it traverses a reverse skein of tubes called veins, not moving in spurts as it did in the arteries, but climbing up the legs and down the arms like a lazy brook, picking up debris all the way. Eventually, it flows into an outsized cistern that hangs vertically within the rib cage like an elongated sausage, a well called the *vena cava*. Blood in the vena cava is so dirty that it is of no use whatever. So it must be cleaned. The lungs are the body's scrubbing station.

Which brings us back to the heart. As was said, its right side contains a pump that is attached to but quite separate from the pump that drives the general circulation. This right-side pump circulates dirty blood from the vena cava into and through the lungs and returns its corpuscles, cleansed and full of fresh oxygen to the left-side pump.

And the cycle begins again.

The wonders never cease. Common knowledge holds that a man has but one heart. Science knows he has three. The second heart is not an organ but a conglomerate of all the muscles of your limbs through which your veins run as they climb back toward the heart. How, for instance, can a distant heart lift blood from the ankles to the chest? The beat of the heart is far away now. Well, nature has caused veins to run through and between muscles which, by their movements of contraction and relaxation, squeeze those veins with repeated milking actions that inches their contents upward and along the homebound freeway. But a drop of blood has weight, and gravity pulls it earthward. Why doesn't it slide back down the ice-slick vein? Nature has inserted valves into every vertical vein to catch the blood and hold it until another muscular squeeze can urge it on to the next valve. And that complex of valves is your second heart, if the word can be defined as anything that moves blood along its circuit.

Your third heart is a powerful double-domed muscle called the diaphragm. It forms the roof of your abdominal cavity and the floor of your rib cage. It is primarily a breathing muscle, helping to lift the ribs and chest upward for inhalation. It does this by a gigantic contraction that elevates its dome. In raising the dome, it compresses the chest's big cistern of dirty blood, forcing a spillout over the top into the beating heart's right chambers. Thus the heart-to-heart circuit is completed, not because of one incomparable organ but because of three never-resting entities composed of the heart, the arm and leg muscle and the diaphragm, which delivers the final push to the bloodstream.

What has all this to do with diving?

The only means by which your muscles obtain food and oxygen is your circulation. You can dive successfully only when both are abundantly present in your blood. When they are present in your blood, they can be transferred to your cells only by the rhythmic contraction of your muscles. You can dive deep and long and confidently only when your muscles can hold their tone (slight contraction) all day long, and when there is a reserve of endurance available for the inevitable crises a diver encounters.

You can buy your air in tanks and feel confident of its quality. But the quality of performance as you use that air depends on your circulation. And the quality of your circulation depends on your muscles. Never forget this! Muscles are a do-it-yourself product. That's what all this has to do with happy diving.

3

Start Where You Are

If you want to dive, those who bear the responsibility of introducing you to and training you for the sport will have definite expectations. Or call them standards of eligibility.

Right off, your instructors will want to know about your swimming skills. They will be deeply concerned about your health. Your lifestyle will be of intense interest. Finally, they will want assurance of your self-discipline and common sense. The road to certification is not easy.

As a would-be diver, you also must be concerned about your qualifications. You too need to be concerned about these issues, and you must have the conviction, partly intellectual and partly emotional, that you really can hack it.

For instance, what is your reply to these questions: Is my swimming ability realy up to par? Do I have the physical endurance to succeed as an underwater diver? In case of an emergency, facing a life-or-death decision, will I push the panic button?

Your request for certification may be made to one of several large professional diving associations, each of which has developed its own performance code and its own system of grading. It is amazing that although there are no universal standards, their codes resemble each other to an astonishing degree. Let's look at some of their criteria.

SWIMMING SKILLS

One of the first organizations to support the sport of skin and scuba diving with a scientifically based course of instruction was the YMCA. It might be fairly said that their sponsorship, through their many swimming pools and professional instructors, put the idea across.

Over the years, their experiences with the men and women they taught to dive were welded into a body of knowledge that assured enjoyment of the sport and the safety of the participant. Those experiences are now a part of the doctrine of the American Standards Committee on Underwater Safety, whose swimming test is widely accepted as an accurate measure of necessary swimming skill.

The test requires first that an applicant be fifteen years of age or older. There is no upper age limit.

Second, an individual must be able to swim two-hundred yards without fins in less than six minutes.

Third, the individual must be able to stay afloat or tread water for ten minutes without using accessories.

Fourth, it is desirable that an applicant have completed training for either a junior or a senior lifesaving certificate, or lacking that, have demonstrated the ability and discipline to complete such a course.

Another certifying group is the Professional Association of Diving Instructors (PADI) which is probably the largest association of its kind in the world. It asks its students to meet five criteria:

Swim two-hundred yards using two or more strokes.

Swim forty feet underwater on a single breath of air.

Dive to a depth of eight or ten feet, recover a five-pound weight, and bring it to the surface.

Tread water for five minutes.

Float or bob (drownproof) with a minimum amount of movement for at least five minutes.

Other schools of thought ask for somewhat more or less. One authority insists that a candidate swim fifty yards while carrying ten pounds of lead on a weight belt. Another requires a student to float for ten minutes without moving. A standard textbook says an applicant should be able to swim three-hundred yards using the crawl, side, and breast strokes.

Two other major agencies offering certification in scuba are NAUI (National Association of Underwater Instructors) and NASDS (National Association of Scuba Diving Schools). These two associations, like the YMCA and PADI, have trained thousands of students of all ages in safe and enjoyable sport diving.

"There is no short cut. Good swimming ability is a must," say scuba authors Craig and Dehn. On the other hand, some experts are convinced that advanced swimming skills are not all that necessary.

The Underwater Explorers' Society, located in Freeport, Bahamas, is one of the world's best equipped diving resorts. Run by physicians, it has conducted nine annual seminars for aquadocs for many years, that earn credits from the American Medical Association. Their attitude is that "three hours is enough to train anybody, any age, to make an open water dive." They teach a beginners' course daily, according to reports, and have introduced over 30,000 novices to the sport.

The first step is a poolside lecture, followed by a session in their shallow pool to learn essential techniques. Next the students move to the seven-foot training pool, and then to the eighteen-foot, where pressure equalization is practiced. The lesson ends with class and instructor taking a boat ride to a nearby shallow reef for a genuine open water experience.

If students enjoy it and want to qualify as divers, the society then offers a certification course consisting of thirty hours of classroom, pool, and open water instruction. Their safety record is extraordinary.

But by and large, the mass of expert opinion advocates better-than-average swimming skills. "You better be better than average," one instructor insists. Another says, "You need to be comfortable and relaxed in the water, so you must be reasonably proficient."

What is reasonably proficient?

Each applicant must decide the answer to that question for himself, remembering that swimming is only part of the art. One professional wraps it up in a sentence: "If you are endowed with a mature, healthy body and mind and possess a measure of swimming ability and common sense, there is no reason why you cannot learn to dive with the best of them, regardless of age, background, or athletic prowess."

Obviously, this is a sport that a Marc Spitz can enjoy, but so can an average guy.

HEALTH

Good health is an essential part of underwater safety. Both YMCA and professional instructor groups require a medical examination and a physician's approval for participation.

Because the sport is still new, most physicians know little about it. To fill this lack, a handbook for physicians called *The Merck Manual* offers a useful protocol that makes these points:

Persons who are grossly obese have a low tolerance for exercise and are susceptible to decompression sickness. Scuba divers should not be obese.

Age limits may be disregarded, but older candidates should have strong hearts and efficient lungs.

The body's air spaces (sinuses, middle ear, Eustacian tube) must readily equalize air pressures. No single chamber may be blocked off. If air is trapped in a head-space, it can lead to trouble on ascent from a dive.

Airways to the paranasal sinuses (accessory to the nose) should be clear. Their blockage or that of the middle ear space can have serious consequences.

Chronic nasal congestion, a perforated ear drum, or "certain otological procedures"—meaning some kinds of ear operations—are contraindications to diving.

Diving should be avoided during colds, asthma, or hay fever attacks, or whenever the membrane that lines the nose is inflamed.

Epileptic seizures or fainting attacks and brittle diabetes "speak strongly" against diving. So does addiction to alcohol or drugs.

Any medication that causes drowsiness or diminished alertness is undesirable.

Lack of emotionsl stability is perilous. A perceptive physician may be able to deduce it from an applicant's "inappropriate motivation, a history of impulsive behavior, or accident proneness."

Pregnancy presents unknown hazards, especially from the standpoint of decompression injury to the fetus. (Preggies are advised not to dive.)

If individuals persist in diving despite medical contraindications, they should be clearly informed of the risks involved, and the physician should make his disapproval a matter of record.

Note that the vast majority of American sportsmen and women continue to be eligible.

Other authorities, who are veteran instructors, make the same points in more direct language.

Never dive with a cold. Or a sinus infection.

Be sure your heart and lungs are capable of hard work.

Your vision needs to be good, at least 20-30.

Don't accept students who have fainting spells, blackouts, fears, or show a tendency to panic.

Drink no alcohol within *eight* hours prior to a dive.

Take neither sleeping pills nor medication that induces drowsiness.

One author-diver, formerly an associate of Jacques Cousteau, arbitrarily rules out applicants who are psychotic, epileptic, diabetic, or tubercular, and persons with heart or lung disease. But who wouldn't! For them to dive, he says moderately, would be "unwise."

What is obvious in this review is that all persons reponsible for the good name of scuba diving are trying to weed out participants who might damage themselves. The unwell and the diseased are a small minority. What remains, then, is what psychologists call the "human factor."

LIFESTYLE AND COMMON SENSE

As a prospective candidate for certification, you had better take a good look at yourself. Your instructor is going to, so it might be wise to beat him to it. Safe diving demands that a diver be responsible. Unfortunately, this quality is not highly praised in today's push-button society. TV interviews and *People*-type magazines apparently delight in exhibiting freaks and fanatics. Insulated from most kinds of disasters, modern citizens seldom have to make life-or-death decisions. Exploring the underworld of rivers lakes, and sea confronts them with reality.

Scuba instructors welcome students who are trapped by neither alcohol nor drugs, who take care of their clothes, their cars, and their bodies. Instructors applaud such traits as thoughtfulness, courtesy, and dependability, particularly the last. In every way possible, they try to develop a feeling of selflessness and concern for others. Not that every scuba diver must become a knight in shining tanks; but in a buddy dive, he is responsible for someone else's life. It is a unique and frequently stressful assignment.

Good judgement under pressure is essential. Before allowing anyone to take your measurements for a dry suit, explore your motivation for becoming a diver. Is it to gain admiration, to impress someone, or to show off in a romantic setting? If your answer is yes to any of these, better pack it in; the moment you don a scuba tank, you become an endangered species.

On the other hand, if you want to discover unimaginable marvels and witness sights that only a few of the world's population will ever see, and if you want to grow mentally, physically, and spiritually, then diving is for you. If your secret yearning is simply the result of that age-old thrust that sent Livingstone to Africa and Columbus to the New World, you are on the right track. You can say, with the Norwegian explorer Nansen that "Man wants to know what lies beyond the far horizon, and when he stops wanting to know, he stops being a man."

Mortals live by codes rooted in reality. As children, most of us were taught the rules of human behavior in a divine document called the Ten Commandments. In the early popularity of skin and scuba diving, Edward H. Lanphier, now a clergyman as well as a physician-member of the department of Preventive Medicine at the University of Wisconsin, put together an inventory of rules for diving. He called it "Ten Commandments for Safe Diving."

Since its first appearance in *The New Science of Skin and Scuba Diving**, thousands of enthusiasts have lived by it. As you read it, measure your own capacity to accept its precepts. It is an exacting program.

Ten Commandments for Safe Diving.

1. *Be fit.* Have a medical check-up. Be a good swimmer.
2. *Get Good Training.* Reading a book is not enough; enroll in a good course. Learn the facts and procedures of safe diving.
3. *Have Good Equipment.* Be careful about bargains and don't build it yourself. Keep your equipment in top condition; check it before every dive. Use only tested and approved equipment. Refrain from alterations or untrained adjustment of equipment.
4. *Never Dive Alone.* Always have a buddy with you under water. Have a tender at the surface whenever possible.
5. *Know the Diving Area.* Avoid dangerous places and poor conditions. Take whatever special precautions the area requires.
6. *Use a Boat, Float, or Both.* Fly the diver's flag. Be able to reach safety fast. If motorboats are in the area, surface only close to your diver's flag and with caution. Wear an inflatable vest.
7. *Plan Your Dive.* Solve the problem in advance. Know decompression rules. Keep track of depth and time. Stick to your plan.
8. *Be Ready for Emergencies.* Have plans of action ready. Know lifesaving, first aid, and rescue breathing. Have first aid equipment. Have a diver's ID card. Know the location of the nearest compression chamber.

*Council for National Cooperation in Aquatics, Piscataway, N.J.: New Century Publishers, Inc., 1980.

9. *Beware of Breath-Holding.* With SCUBA, breath continuously throughout the dive; exhale all the way up in an emergency ascent. Without
   SCUBA, avoid excessive over-breathing before skin dives; don't over
   exert; don't push your limit on breath-holding.
10. *Get Medical Attention.* IF ANY ABNORMALITY DEVELOPS
    DURING OR AFTER A DIVE. Don't waste time; don't try to "drown
    the problem." Wear your ID card after any dive that might
    cause bends.

Several more commandments are also in order, gleaned from
the experts.

Stay in top condition.

Join a good diving club.

Practice skin diving before trying to learn scuba diving.

Get your training from a certified instructor or agency, never
from a friend.

Eat right and get plenty of rest.

Have your scuba gear serviced annually.

If you don't know the dive site or the weather conditions and
current conditions, ask the locals.

To keep up to date, dive at least a dozen times a year.

Never loan your equipment to an untrained individual.

Never try to train another person. Leave it to a pro.

If you feel weak or tired, scrub the dive.

If you haven't dived for months, give yourself a refresher course
in a pool

Keep your legs in shape by swimming at least one-half mile with
fins and snorkel three times a week.

Always practice buddymanship. The life *he* saves may be your
own.

Can you live with those terms? If you can, you are ready for the
next step of your self-examination. It will consist of a series of spot
checks on your personal fitness, not necessarily for glamorous
blue-water expeditions, but for the serious business of facing the
heartaches and ailments—yes, and the joys—of everyday life.

TESTS FOR FUN AND FITNESS

The tests of yesteryear were generally designed to test strength.
A favorite sport was the tug of war. To possess powerful muscles
was every boy's dream. Today's tests look elsewhere. Speed and
endurance are the twin pillars supporting heroes of the diamond,
gridiron, and basketball court. And the source of those qualities is
the human heart.

These tests examine the heart, not with complete precision but
with enough accuracy to reveal the presence of clinkers in your

furnace. Gathered from a lifetime of examining the research studies of many human-performance laboratories, they will lead you
to a better understanding of your own prowess.

First, do you know how to take your own pulse? Few people do.
Instead, they usually go to a doctor's office where a nurse makes
that simple measurement. The pulse rate, however, is the easiest
and most accurate indication of the heart's condition.

You might begin by putting your ear to a friend's chest. You'll
hear a lub-dub sound, repeating itself over and over—about
seventy times per minute in males, about eighty in females, and
still faster in children. Each lub-dub represents a *beat* or contraction of the heart's left ventricle. The sound is the result of a
quantity of fast-moving blood colliding with the tail of the stream
pumped out by the previous contraction. The number of those
beats per minute tells an important part of the heart's story. The
rate at which it *accelerates* during work tells still more. The
promptness with which it slows down after work can indicate
good news or bad. For all those reasons, you need to know how to
take your pulse.

Try it like this.

1. Sit comfortably beside a kitchen (or any other) table or in a
   chair with your right forearm resting palm up either on the
   table top or on your thigh.
2. Reach across your body with your free hand and place your
   first three fingers on the inner side of your wrist about one
   and one-half inches from the notch where your wrist enlarges
   to become a hand and about one-quarter of the distance from
   the upper margin of the wrist to its lower edge.
3. Press the fingers gently into the "groove" that you should be
   able to feel between the ligaments that run from forearm to
   hand. What you are looking for is a movement (sort of bump)
   beneath the skin that repeats itself over and over. That
   movement is your pulse, and you should count it from time
   to time as long as you live if you want a quick check of
   your heart.
4. Count those pulses. How often do they occur in each minute?
   If you have better things to do, a shortcut is available. Count
   the beats to ten seconds and multiply by six. Nurses say they
   find it easier to count the beats for fifteen seconds and multiply by four. They never explain why.

If you are counting pulse beats following an exercise period, you
might try your carotid pulse. The arteries that feed blood to your

head are called carotid arteries. They run up each side of the neck to where the sloping jawbone angles upward toward the ear. If your heart is pounding, your carotid is pulsing. After exercising, the carotid pulse is easier to find than the wrist pulse. Simply press an exploratory finger along the jawbone toward the ear and you'll surely find it. But be careful never to press both sides of the neck at the same time. It stops the flow of blood to the brain and can cause a fainting spell.

A QUICK TEST FOR HEART STRENGTH

A diver's body must function perfectly no matter which end is up. On occasions of zero visibility, it is easy to become disoriented. But the heart always knows and responds according to its fitness.

This test, which warns of what doctors call orthostatic unfitness, is easy to perform. Orthostatic is a word pertaining to the erect body as opposed to the recumbent body. When one is standing, the heart is forced to work harder pumping blood against gravity to the head and shoulders and into the arms. While one is lying down, arms, legs, organs, and heart are on approximately the same level, so the heart's work doesn't have to fight gravity. The difference can be measured by counting the heart's acceleration when the body first stands after one gets out of bed.

Physiologists who have used this test know that a strong heart accepts the change from a horizontal to vertical position without much fuss. A weak heart, on the other hand, may begin to race like a hot rod engine at the start of a drag race. What does your own heart do?

1. Lie down quietly for several minutes to permit your heart to assume its normal, relaxed, resting rate.
2. Count your pulse for one minute.
3. Rise without hurry and stand erect, doing nothing for a full minute. Then take your pulse for the next minute.
4. Your rate while standing should be higher than your resting rate. Subtract the resting rate from the standing rate. The difference represents your heart's secret message. A bit of background may help here. Mass experiments by scientists determined that an average adult's resting rate is seventy-four beats per minute whereas his average standing rate is ninety-two beats per minute. That's a difference of twenty beats (92 − 72 = 20). Is that good or bad?

To find out, scientists also tested hundreds of athletes who obviously had developed healthy, fit hearts. They learned that an athlete's heart would beat, on the average, from six to ten beats faster when he moved from a horizontal position to a perpendicular.

Physiologists concluded that anyone's heart may be unfit, regardless of age, if its rate increases by more than six to ten beats per minute between lying down and standing.

Do this test at least twice and record the result. What is your lying–standing difference? Whatever it is, it's a message straight from the heart.

HERE'S A QUICKIE (TESTING RECUPERATIVE POWER)

1. Take your pulse sitting.
2. Walk up a flight of stairs, not fast, not slowly, just as is your habit.
3. Count your pulse beats per minute.

After such stress, a fit heart should be beating about ninety beats per minute.

An unfit heart is indicated by any figure higher than ninety beats per minute after climbing one flight of stairs. Incidentally, its pace can soar to 150 or better. If your count is over ninety, dedicate yourself to a program that gives your heart what it needs. What it needs is a regular, rhythmic, fifteen-to-thirty minute overload of exercise at least four times each week, plus tender loving care.

THE GOLDING ONE-MINUTE STEP TEST

Testing heart strength by asking a person to step up and down on a stool has a long history of experimentation. The most famous (and hardest) test was developed years ago in the fatigue laboratory at Harvard University. It required a subject to step onto a twenty-inch bench thirty times a minute for five minutes. Fitness was judged by the duration of stepping (many subjects could complete only a couple of minutes) and the subsequent heart rate after one minute of rest. Harvard students failed by the thousands.

A shorter test, which also appraises leg and heart strength, was developed more recently at Kent State University by Dr. Lawrece Golding. His test has been widely used, and his scoring table has helped innumerable unfit Americans.

Why not try it?

Obtain a kitchen chair with a solid seat or a stool and set it in an open space.

A watch or clock with a second hand must be available so you

can maintain a cadence of one upward step every two seconds—
thirty steps for the one-minute duration of the test.

1. Step up on the chair with the right foot and bring the left foot
   alongside to the chair seat.
2. Step down from the chair with the right foot first and bring
   the left foot to the floor alongside.
3. Repeat this cycle thirty times in sixty seconds.
4. Sit down and do nothing for fifteen seconds.
5. Take your pulse for fifteen seconds and record the figure; skip
   fifteen seconds; take your pulse for a second span of fifteen
   seconds and record the count; skip fifteen seconds. Take
   your pulse for a third span of fifteen seconds, and record
   that count.
6. Relax. The hard work is finished.

You now have before you three pulse counts. Add them up. Their
total is a pretty good reflection of you compared to others. Refer to
Table 1, which applies to unconditioned subjects, to ascertain if
you are above average, average, or below average.

If you are merely average or below average, that judgment
probably also applies to your likely enjoyment of skin or scuba
diving. To get the most fun out of any sport, one's fitness should
certainly be better than average.

Note: This exercise tests three aspects of your fitness: heart
muscle strength, thigh muscle strength, and the arterial system
by which the heart delivers oxygenated blood to working muscles.

If you have performed this test, you now have a figure reflecting
the use of your right leg to step up onto a chair. But diving is
a two-legged business. How about your left leg? Is it weaker?
Stronger? The same? You can find out, within rough limits, by
doing the same test, stepping up and down on the same chair
using the left leg.

Add up your three left-leg counts and compare their total with
the right-leg total. If they match, you are well-balanced in quadriceps strength. If one leg is obviously stronger than the other, you
might find yourself swimming in a circle without knowing it.
More important, you now know which leg to strengthen, but we
tackle that problem in another chapter.

Three other elements of fitness need to be investigated to learn
where you stand as a candidate for maximum diving enjoyment.
They are agility, shoulder and arm strength, and explosive power
of the body's chief locomotive muscles, the thighs.

Let's test them one at a time.

Table 1. Pulse Beat Scores (Sum of Three) for Unconditioned Subjects

Above average	51 to 74
Average	77 to 100
Below average	104 & higher

Physiologists working on university campuses often need to test hundreds of students in as short a time as possible. In consequence, they seek endlessly for a single exercise that will measure most of the factors that add up to fitness. Years ago, a man named Burpee decided he had discovered just such an activity, which he called the Burpee Thrust. It has since helped to measure the agility of American soldiers and sailors in two world wars. It assumes that you possess one quality on which you must make your own judgment. It assumes that you have a strong heart.

Here is the test.

1. Take your standing pulse rate.
2. Place a stop watch or a clock with a second hand within easy visual range.
3. Timing yourself, go through the position changes (stand—squat—thrust—squat—stand) four times as rapidly as you can. Take each position correctly and without delaying. Note the total time elapsed for the sixteen moves. (Counting them aloud may help your concentration.
4. Check your score from Table 2 or 3. Read across the top and find your age group. Read down the column for your age group to your elapsed time. A score of 50 points (left hand column) indicates average ability.

Table 2. Burpee Thrust Tables for Men

	Seconds			
Score	Ages 15–25	Ages 26–35	Ages 36–45	Age 46 and above
100	5.5	6.5	7.5	8
90	5.5	6.5	7.5	8
80	6	7	8	9
70	7	8	9	10
60	7	9	9	11
50	8	10	10–11	12–13
40	9	11–12	12	14–16
30	10	13	13–14	17–18
20	11	14–15	15–16	19–20
10	12	16	17	21
0	13	17	18	22

Table 3. Burpee Thrust Tables for Women

Score	Seconds			
	Ages 15–25	Ages 26–35	Ages 36–45	Age 46 and above
100	7	7	7.5	
90	7	7	8	10–11
80	7	8	9	12
70	8	9	10–11	13
60	9	10	12	14
50	10	11	13	15–16
40	11	12	14	17
30	12	13–14	15–16	18
20	14–15	15–16	17	19
10	16	17	18	20–21
0	17	18	19–20	22

Read across the top and find your age group. Read down the column for your age group to your elapsed time. A score of 50 points (left hand column) indicates average ability.

PULL-UPS TEST

A scuba diver's power is in his thighs, which is to say in his fins. A snorkeler's power is double ended, in his fins and in his arms and shoulders. The one best test that reveals the strength of arms and shoulders for the crawl, side, breast, and backstrokes is the pull-up. It is simple, brief, and easily scored. Men pull themselves up on any overhead bar until the chin is on a level with the bar and they repeat the move as many consecutive times as they can. Women, being weaker in arm and shoulder muscles, are scored by their hanging time, during which they suspend themselves, feet off the ground, for as many seconds as possible. It sounds easy, but it isn't.

To find your score, refer to Table 4 for men and Table 5 for women.

SARGENT'S CHALK JUMP

Part of fitness is the body's explosive power. A baseball pitcher "explodes" his arm and shoulder muscles when he throws his fast ball at better than one-hundred miles per hour. A high jumper "explodes" his leg muscles when he lifts himself up and over a seven-foot high jump. A good diver has no need to explode. His instructors ask him to contain his power so that his heart

Table 4. Pull-Up Table for Men

	Number of pull-ups			
Score	Ages 15–25	Ages 26–35	Ages 36–45	Age 46 and older
100	18.5	20	13	9.5
90	18	19	13	9
80	17–16	18–17	12–11	9
70	15–14	16–14	10–9	8
60	13–11	13–11	8–7	7
50	10–8	10–8	6–5	6–5
40	7	7–6	4	4
30	5–4	5–4	3	3
20	3–2	3–2	2	2
10	1	1	1	1

Table 5. Arm-Hanging Time for Women

	Seconds of hanging			
Score	Ages 15–25	Ages 26–35	Ages 36–45	Age 46 or older
100	109	97	93	71
90	105	95	92–90	70–65
80	100	90–85	85–80	60–55
70	90–80	75–65	70–60	50
60	70–60	55–45	50–40	40
50	50–40	35	35–30	30
40	30	30–25	25–20	20–15
30	20	20–15	15	10
20	10	10	10–8	7–5
10	5–3	5–3	5–3	3

rate remains steady and his breathing slow. Nevertheless, explosive power translates into reserve power. A body capable of exploding is a body capable of swimming for hour after hour of aerobic comfort. So we present a final test—that of explosive power. Physiologists call it Sargent's Chalk Jump, naming it in honor of the physical educator who first made it important in measuring fitness.

In essence, it is a standing high jump from which the elements of skill have been stripped. It measures in inches the vertical distance above the earth that both sets of leg muscles, working in unison, can lift the weight of your body.

All you need is a wall and a piece of chalk.

Table 6. Sargent's Chalk Jump for Men

Score	Inches jumped			
	Ages 15–25	Ages 26–35	Ages 36–45	Age 46 and over
100	26.5	25.2	25	19
90	26	25	24	18
80	25	24	23	17–16
70	23–20	23–22	22–21	15–14
60	22–21	21–19	20–18	13
50	20–18	18–16	16–14	9–7
40	17–14	14	12–10	7–6
30	12–10	12–8	8–6	5–4
20	8–6	6	4–3	3–2

Table 7. Sargent's Chalk Jump for Women

Score	Inches jumped			
	Ages 15–25	Ages 26–35	Ages 36–45	Age 46 or over
100	18	16	14	11.8
90	18	16	14	11
80	17	15	13	10
70	16–15	14–13	12	9
60	14	12	11–10	8–7
50	13–12	11–9	9–8	6–5
40	10–8	8–6	7–5	4
30	6	5–4	4	3–2
20	4–3	3–2	3–2	1

1. Stand flat-footed alongside a wall, your shoulder touching it lightly.
2. Take a piece of chalk (a magic marker won't rub off) and reach overhead as high as possible and make a light mark on the wall. That mark records your reach.
3. Crouch and spring upward (or use whatever style you favor) and make a mark at the very top of your leap. That is your jump-mark.

The difference between your reach mark and your jump mark is the measure of your explosive power.

Three trials are allowed. Record your best jump and check your score in Table 6 for men or Table 7 for women. If it is below 50, your legs need regular workouts.

THE COOPER TEST

When Dr. Ken Cooper, author of *Aerobics* and other seminal works on fitness, was in the United States Air Force, he was ordered to test young airmen by the battalion. So he invented a procedure that he reported in his first book. He simply took them onto a parade ground, hundreds of them, and told them to run for twelve minutes. It was easy to score. If an airman ran one and one-half miles in twelve minutes, he passed. If he ran less, he flunked.

When compared with standard tests using oxygen consumption, Cooper's test stood up.

Guidances:
Don't smoke before the test.
Don't eat for two hours before the test.
Stretch and warm up before you begin the run.
Cool down and don't stand around afterwards.

Ratings for Fitness
Time: running for 12 minutes.
Less than 1 mile   Very poor condition indicated
1.00-1.24 miles   Poor
1.24-1.49 miles   Fair
1.50-1.74 miles   Good
1.75 or more miles   Excellent.*

Once you take these tests, you will know where you are with greater certainty than ever before. Chances are, you will not be entirely satisfied with yourself. Maybe your physique is not quite as robust as you would wish.

Well, there is an answer. In Chapter 4, you will learn how to mend your weaknesses, whether they are related specifically to the sport of diving or to the equally difficult art of living. Improvement is within reach if you choose to seek it.

*From *The Aerobics Way,* by Kenneth H. Cooper, M.D., New York: M. Evans and Company, 1977.

4

Conditioning Drills to Improve Your Skills

American swimming coaches have devised a thousand different ways to improve the speed of competitive swimmers. So far as we know, few have studied the problems of long, slow underwater swimming. Physiologists have written books about the muscles that are the body's principal movers, but none has studied the dynamics of those same muscles when they are encumbered by flippers, wet suits, and scuba tanks.

This chapter is an effort to understand the problems of the scuba enthusiast and make recommendations that may increase his prowess and expand his enjoyment of the sport.

According to surveys, the difficulties of beginners (as well as veterans) usually manifest themselves as tired ankles, weary knees, even aching jaws. Clearly, their most active muscles give out long before their bottom time expires. Those muscles obviously need conditioning. Hereunder, you will find the most common of these spot enfeeblements described and a brief program of isometric conditioning suggested, which if directions are followed, should provide a pain-free performance.

Instead of suffering from localized weaknesses, some divers experience a general malaise and a feeling of gutlessness. A toning-up program is needed for them, one that will recharge the total physique. Some call it endurance conditioning. The details of successful endurance programs are outlined later in this chapter.

Which should come first: attention to inadequate muscles or attention to an inadequate body? The choice presented here results from the conviction that almost any body is adequate for scuba diving, provided it is equipped with certain skills.

On the other hand, spot strength improvement can raise the level of enjoyment almost immediately, thereby maintaining one's interest. To that end, these exercises are suggested.

Two additional preliminary steps are needed. The first is to acquire an understanding of how muscles work. The second is to practice a relatively new but effective form of muscle reconditioning called isometrics.

ISOMETRICS

Skipping the big words and complicated explanations, accept the proposition that the muscles with which we are concerned have only two principal functions:

1. To open a joint.
2. To close a joint.

Curl one hand into a fist. Now slowly point the forefinger. Note that it is straight! Your finger muscles have *opened* not one but three of its joints to straighten or extend that finger. Muscles that open joints are called extensors.

Curl your forefinger back into the fist. A different set of finger muscles has now *closed* the three joints. Those muscles are called flexors.

All your muscles are either extensors or flexors, although a few are both.

Generally, muscles are paired so each flexor has an extensor as its partner. They are generally located on opposite sides of a bone, opposing each other. The bone moves only because one of those paired muscles contracts. Obviously, only one member of the pair can contract at a time. The other must be relaxed.

When muscles won't perform (contract) as powerfully or for as long a time as required, they must be conditioned. Various training methods have been devised. Lifting weights is one form of training. Isometrics is another.

Experience has shown that muscles' cells grow larger and stronger only when they are vigorously stimulated. In other words, the greater the intensity of effort, the more the muscles are stimulated. One method succeeds through the use of bar bells, weights, and muscle-building machines.

Isometric training is better suited to our purpose and requires no special equipment. If you are not aware of the magical power of isometrics to recondition underdeveloped muscles, listen to some of those who have profited.

Dr. Francis Drury, a professor of physical education at Louisiana State University, once said of isometrics, "It could be put to work on any part of the body you want to slim, develop, or reapportion. And because of this, the use of IC (isometric contraction) requires only seconds a day to accomplish specific results."

Dr. James E. Counsilman, the celebrated olympic swimming coach from Indiana University, used isometrics to help train himself for a successful personal test, swimming the English Channel even though he was a senior citizen. He said, "A 98-pound weakling can go into an isolation cell with only four walls and bars on the window and come out a 200-pound monster."

An informal survey produced such statements as the following:

"It added 15 yards to my drive."

"It gave me a much faster serve."

"I play piano concerts night after night. They don't tire me any more."

How can anyone make such claims? Because two German scientists named Muller and Hettinger experimented for years with muscle cells, seeking answers to the riddle of muscular power. What they found was amazing. They announced their discovery with these words: "A muscle gains strength if it is contracted at least up to one-half of its potential total strength, provided that this contraction is maintained about one-fifth of the time required for that muscle to reach complete fatigue, and provided that this contraction is performed at least once every day."

Almost nobody believed them. All over the world, scientists in human performance laboratories set out to prove them wrong. But their theory worked. When a muscle cell is stimulated it reacts in some unknown fashion and becomes larger and stronger. Recently, slight modifications have been suggested. Some scientists say that growth begins when a contraction is only one-third of a muscle's potential. Others state that three contractions per day build bodies faster than one. But the principle remains unshaken.

Isometrics offers the easiest, fastest means of building fitness for diving ever discovered. But remember this: No system produces instant fitness. All improvement must be progressive, a little bit each day, the improvement curve sometimes pausing on brief plateaus before beginning another climb.

Overload is also necessary. Overload is asking your muscles to do more than they want to do.

How can such a system work when it does not use weights or other devices? It works because it pits one muscle against another or a single muscle against itself.

Example of Muscle against Muscle

Assume the conventional attitude of prayer, hands before the chest, palm to palm. Push one hand against the other, hard, right hand opposing the left hand with all the strength of your shoulder muscles. Every muscle involved hardens across the chest, around the shoulders, down the arms, through the wrists and into the hands. That's muscle against muscle. Research in isometrics has revealed that such a push maintained for from six to ten seconds provides all the stimulation needed to cause the muscle cells to enlarge.

Example of Single Muscle Contraction

While seated, place your hand under the top edge of a heavy desk or table. Try to life it. Raise your forearm against the resistence of the desk. Your bicep contracts, becoming as hard as ebony. Ten seconds of that and you have stimulated your bicep to a new level of performance.

As you relax after such intense contraction, you will feel a warm glow suffusing your muscles and enveloping your body. It is the result of blood coursing through channels that were briefly blocked by intense contraction. Now the muscle cells are being cleansed of the waste products they created during their hard labor. Fresh oxygen is entering and reviving them. As the TV ad says, you are "feeling good all under." And the process works through each muscle cell. It mysteriously gives birth to a slight increment of growth. The reason for this is not yet understood by scientists, but it happens.

The United States Marines use isometrics to train new recruits. Even women marines perform an IC series including tummy and thigh tighteners. Our astronauts used IC. So do golfers, including Gary Player, and 137-pound Jerry Barber. So our spot muscle strengthening program will utilize isometric contractions as a training method. It works.

THE TOE POINTER SERIES

How to Measure Ankle Flexibility

To be an efficient and successful free diver, you need flexible ankles.

Toe pointing requires ankle flexibility. Scientists call it plantar flexion. Some people are born with it, some have to acquire it. To which group do you belong? A simple maneuver will provide an answer.

Stand erect with feet together, barefoot or wearing socks. Clasp your hands together behind your neck. Squat into a deep knee-bend, dropping your buttocks as close as possible to your heels without causing them to leave the ground.

If your ankles are flexible, you can drop all the way down without raising the heels.

If your ankles are stiff, you will either topple over backwards or your heels must lift off the floor.

Toe Pointer No 1

Purpose: To improve pointing the toes by stretching some of the ligaments that bind the foot bones to the ankle bones.

Position: Stand about twelve inches from a wall, facing it. Place the toes of the right foot against the base of the wall.

Movement: Lift the right heel and leg, pointing the toes so that the shinbone and the top curve of the instep make a line that is approximately straight. Press the toes and the top of the foot against the wall with enough force to stretch the muscles and sinews on top of the instep. Hold for ten seconds. Relax. Repeat ten times with each foot, four or more times each week.

Comment: Pointing the toes produces the best fin kick for underwater work. Most swimmers' ankles do not need stretching, but all ankles need strengthening. This exercise will benefit all.

Toe Pointer No. 2

Purpose: Same as that of No. 1, to stretch the ankle to facilitate pointing the toes.

Position: Place a pillow on the floor. Kneel on it so that the instep is cushioned when you sit back on your heels.

Movement: With the instep inverted and toes parallel to the floor but cushioned by the pillow, settle back slowly onto your heels, allowing your weight gradually to press down on the ankles so that their tight wrappings of ligaments and muscles are stretched. In time your weight will tend to "open" the ankle. When discomfort or pain becomes excessive, rock forward on your knees and let your ankles rest. Repeat ten times daily, four or more times weekly.

Comment: Men with fat thighs may have difficulty. Remember that any pressure that straightens the instep, pointing the toes, is good only if repeated regularly and with sufficient pressure. Living tissue stretches slowly if you give it a chance. Always stop short of placing so much weight on the heels that a ligament might tear.

Ankle Strengthener No. 1

Purpose: To strengthen the calf muscle, which pulls the toes down and holds them down, thereby pointing them like a ballet dancer's.

Movement: Stand erect, grasp a nearby support to maintain your balance, lift one foot off the floor, and raise your body's weight on the other foot until you are standing on tiptoe, on one foot. Hold the position for a count of ten. Repeat ten times, resting between lifts. Do this exercise at least four days a week. Change feet and repeat.

Comment: As your calf muscle becomes stronger, you may want to stimulate it even more. You can do this while holding a weight in your free hand. Use a ten-pound dumbbell or a small suitcase full of books. Or you can add to your reps (repetitions), moving from ten up to fifteen. Don't hold the lift beyond ten seconds as it will do no good. All improvement comes, says IC theory, within the first six to ten seconds. Skiers should also do this exercise.

Toe Pointer No. 3

Purpose: To stretch the ligaments, tendons, and muscles of the top of the foot in order to increase their flexibility.

Position: Using a cushion, kneel with feet pointed backwards and place the tops of both feet against the floor. Lean backwards and sit on your heels, bracing your body by placing your hands on the floor.

Movement: Raise your hips off your heels until your full body weight is supported only by your arms and your inverted feet. Rock back and forth, moving your weight from arms to feet and back, according to the amount of stretch you desire.

Comment: This movement requires a considerable degree of ankle flexibility. It should not be attempted by swimmers who have stiff ankles. Try another toe pointer exercise first and use this one to complete the exercise.

KNEE PAINS OR PROBLEMS

If your diving expeditions cause the development of any knee pain or weakness, two simple isometric exercises may solve them quickly.

Knee Strengthener No. 1

Objective: To increase the strength of the quadriceps and lesser knee muscles so that the approved straight-leg movement of the flutter kick will be more efficient and less tiring.

Position: Sit in a chair and straighten the leg until it is horizontal. Pull the toes backwards into a hook position.

Movement: Contract or "tense" all of the thigh muscles on the horizontal leg plus other muscles around the knee as hard as you can. The feeling is that of an intense, continuing squeeze. The thigh turns hard, showing the outlines of corded muscles. Hold it for ten seconds. Relax. Repeat the ten-second contraction three times. Change to the other leg. Four days a week is recommended.

Knee Strengthener No. 2

Objective: To strengthen the muscles of the knee.

Position: Use a sofa or some other heavy object under which you can hook your toes while lying on your back. Lie down, face up, so you can tuck your right foot beneath the sofa or whatever. Bend the left knee and slide the left foot back comfortably toward your rump.

Movement: Tuck your right foot securely under the sofa so that it is immovable. Contract the muscles of your upper thigh (quadriceps), lifting as hard as possible against the weight of the heavy sofa. Keep the pressure on for ten seconds. Relax. Repeat three times. Change legs. Do this exercise four times each week.

Comment: A diver's power stroke is the down-stroke of the flutter kick. The down-stroke is the result of the contraction of the heavy thigh muscle called the quadriceps. This muscle originates above the hip at the pelvis, runs down the front of the thigh, crosses the knee joint where it envelopes the knee-cap (patella) and then attaches via tough tendons to the top of the lower leg bone, called the tibia (shin bone). Thus it crosses the hip joint and the knee joint. When you tighten the quadriceps, it holds the entire leg absolutely straight. When the quads are thoroughly conditioned, they turn the difficult straight-legged flutter kick into child's play.

Spare-Time Knee Strengthener No. 3

Position: Sit in a kitchen chair so that your thighs are parallel to the ground and your feet flat on the floor. Place your right hand on your right thigh with the fingers touching the knee cap. Place the left hand on top of the right hand.

Movement: Try to lift the right leg up while holding it down with all the strength of your two arms. As the right thigh's quadriceps tries to rise against the resistance of your arms and shoulders, count slowly to ten seconds. Relax and repeat three times. Change legs. Do this exercise four times a week.

Comment: You can improve your leg strength while watching television, waiting for a stop light to change, or sitting in a movie house. The exercise is absolutely silent and suitable even for use in church during a dull sermon, provided you don't grunt when you apply your muscle power.

Any movement that straightens your leg against resistance brings the quads into play. You might try to invent your own knee extensor exercise.

Like jumping up and down, leaping as high off the ground as you can for ten successive bounds.

Or riding a bike.

Or doing laps with a float board while kicking your way from one end of a pool to the other.

Or jogging up hills.

Or jogging on the level—*backwards.*

But do it, do it, do it! And you'll be a better swimmer and diver.

THE HAMSTRINGS

The back of each thigh is equipped with three mighty muscles called the hamstrings, also called Tom, Dick, and Harry by young medical students. They serve to fix the knees and also to open the hip. The sweep of a diver's upstroke when doing the flutter kick is the result of hamstring power.

Over the years, scientists have discovered that many leg injuries happen when a leg's quadriceps are considerably stronger than its hamstrings. Modern coaches insist that the relative strength of "quads" to "hams" should be approximately sixty to forty. In other words, if the maximum lifting power of the quadriceps is sixty pounds, then the hamstrings should be able to lift at least forty pounds.

Pulled hamstrings afflict many track athletes who have such an imbalance. Skiers, skaters, and cyclists, who almost never straighten their legs, usually have hamstrings almost as powerful as their quads. Athletes playing at basketball, soccer, football, and track must straighten their legs, sometimes with such great force that a spindle of muscles will tear in a hamstring's center or "belly" or where it is attached to the bone.

So what should one do? The hamstring must be strengthened.

Hamstring Strengthener No. 1

Objective: To employ isometric contractions of the hamstring muscles to increase their strength.

Position: Sit in a straight chair, ankles crossed with the right ankle in front of the left. Plant the sole of the left foot solidly against the floor so it cannot be moved easily.

Movement: Contract the hamstrings of the right thigh, pulling back the right ankle, resisting with the left. Exert your maximum strength for about ten seconds. Repeat the contraction three times. Recross your ankles, placing the left leg in front, and repeat the routine. Do this at least four times each week.

Comment: This exercise exerts most of its pressure on the lower part of the rather long trio of quadriceps muscles. A slight problem is involved, in that the leg that resists is also being developed. If you are trying to bring up the power of a weak set of hamstrings, this may not be the exercise for you. Try No. 2 instead.

Hamstring Strengthener No. 2

Objective: To strengthen the top section of the hamstrings where the muscle acts to hold the thigh and body in a firm, straight line.

Position: Lie on your back on a bed or pad, legs straight. Cross the right leg over the left so that the ankles are in contact.

Movement: Relax the left or lower leg, using it as a cushion as you contract the hamstrings at the back of the right thigh. With all the strength you can summon, force the leg straight down onto the left ankle and toward the floor. Hold the tension for ten seconds, and relax. Repeat through three contractions. Recross legs with the left on top. Repeat the same routine. Four times or more each week is recommended.

Comment: The position of the bottom leg as it rests on the floor or mattress eliminates the need for its muscles to struggle against the pressure of the active leg. Hence, this exercise will strengthen only the active leg.

Hamstring Strengthener No. 3

Objective: To use your buddy to help strengthen your hamstrings.

Position: Lie face down across a bench, desk, table, or kitchen chair so that the edge comes beneath your hips. Let one leg down until the foot touches the floor. Straighten the other leg until it is horizontal, foot pointed. Ask your buddy to stand beside the elevated foot with his hands on your heel.

Movement: Ask your buddy to push the heel gently toward the floor, gradually increasing the pressure. Simultaneously, contract the hamstrings of the elevated leg to prevent it from being moved. Try to reach a degree of pressure in which your muscular contraction holds your leg on a horizontal plane despite the force he exerts. Continue for ten seconds. Relax. Repeat three times. Change legs and repeat. For maximum results, do this four or more times each week.

Comment: This is one of the best of the strengtheners. As you try the exercise, you can decide to stabilize your leg at various angles from the hips, thereby involving a greater number of muscle spindles and stimulating their growth. Increased strength at various points along the curve of contraction adds power to most swimming kicks. In case your buddy wonders how hard he should press, or if you are uncertain of how strongly you should resist in order to reap the maximum benefit, the answer is that any contraction that uses one-third or more of a muscle's overall strength is bound to produce muscle results.

THE SHOULDERS

A girdle of muscles surrounds the socket in which the head of the humerus (upper arm bone) is seated. Individual muscles are layered and levered around the shoulder's front, side, and back in a way that continues to confound bridge builders. Consider the mechanics of the whirling-dervish strokes of a butterfly swimmer or the compact, splash-chop of the crawl. No engineer ever designed a more efficient machine or a sytem of belts and pulleys so perfectly attuned to the omnidirectional and rotational flow of the arm's forces.

Here, muscles work together in pairs, trios, and whole constellations as they do nowhere else in the body. Here, the strength of one augments the strength of another until the whole is greater than the sum of its individual powers. Fortunately, this eases conditioning. Again, we prefer isometrics as our method. Our only conditioning machines are a kitchen table and chair.

Shoulder Strengthener Series No. 1

Objective: This series of contractions is designed to stimulate many of the front, side, and back muscles of your shoulder girdle.

Position: Sit erect on a kitchen chair, your feet flat on the floor and about four inches apart. Grasp the chair seat, with the fingers beneath it.

Movement 1: Pull upward on the chair seat, using enough strength to force your buttocks hard against the cushion. Hold for ten seconds. Relax and repeat three times.

Movement 2: Slide your hands under your center of gravity and press them down on the edge of the seat, *lifting* your body until you are suspended (or almost so) from your shoulders, which are supported by your arms and hands. Hold for ten seconds. Relax and repeat three times.

Movement 3: Move your feet closer together and extend them an inch or so forward so as to form a brace. Move your hands to the front edge of the chair seat and clasp it by curling your fingers around its front edge.

Brace your legs, lean back slightly, and pull back with your arms and shoulders applying all your strength from front to back. In effect, you are trying to pull your buttocks forward on the chair while simultaneously resisting the movement through your body weight and your braced legs. Hold the shoulder and arm contraction for ten seconds. Relax and repeat three times.

Movement 4: Lean forward until the body assumes an angle of 45 degrees. Hands and feet are positioned as in the previous movement. Contract shoulder and arm muscles as if trying to slide the chair seat backwards under you. (Your weight holds it in place, of course.) Hold for ten seconds. Relax and repeat ten times.

Movement 5: Move your hands to the rear of the chair until your fingers can grasp the chair back at its base. Sitting erect, pull your hands forward so as to press the entire spine hard against the chair back. Hold for ten seconds. Relax and repeat three times.

Movement 6: Flex the hips and lean the body forward. Your feet and hands retain their positions as in Movement 5. Pull hard on the chair back, forcing your rump into the seat. (Note that this movement involves a much larger area of the upper back.) Hold the contraction for ten seconds. Relax and repeat.

Comment: Shoulder girdles are powerful and weak furniture is likely to come unstuck. Be certain that your chair is sturdy enough to withstand your pulls and pushes. If contractions are too intense, this series is a severe test. If you are not comfortable after each exercise, reduce the contraction time to six seconds and the number of repetitions to six. You may also want to modify the intensity of each contraction. Whatever level you establish, continue for a week or two without variation. Four times each week.

As strength increases, you can add to the number of contractions and to their intensity, but not to their length. Six to ten seconds is all the muscles need.

Shoulder Strengthener Series No. 2

Position: Move your chair to a table and sit down as if to eat. Straighten both arms and extend them directly across the table. Drop your outspread hands onto the table top.

Movement 1: Press your hands down with gradually increasing force against the table top. Note that this movement brings your triceps (at the back of your upper arms) into play. Hold your maximum contraction for ten seconds and relax. Repeat three times.

Movement 2: Turn your chair sideways and sit on it with your right side touching the table's edge. Stretch your right arm straight across the table and drop your hand to its surface. Press downward, gently at first and then harder. Hold the press for ten seconds. Relax and repeat three times.

Movement 3: Reverse your chair to face the opposite direction. Stretch your left arm straight across the table and drop your hand to its surface. Press downward, gently at first and then with near-maximum pressure. Hold for ten seconds. Relax and repeat three times.

Shoulder Strengthener Series No. 3

Objective: To stimulate growth in the deltoid muscle, which envelopes the area about the point of each shoulder, as well as its undergrowth of tendons, ligaments, blood vessels, and nerve ganglia. The deltoid is an important muscle, particularly for snorkelers, and it is remarkably easy to condition.

Position: Stand erect in a doorway, feet about twelve inches apart. Place the backs of your hands against the left and right sides of the door frame.

Movement 1: Press outward against the door frame with both hands.

Movement 2: Bend your arms and press the *elbows* outward against the door frame.

Movement 3: Raise the elbows above the head and then press them outward against the door frame.

Comment: Treat each of these three movements like the others, increasing your contraction gradually, holding it for ten seconds, repeating it three times. Four days each week.

Strengthening the weak spots in one's castle walls is always smart. In the excitement of new levels of achievement and security, however, one is apt to forget that the central keep with its armory and granary also needs attention. The body's trunk is your central keep.

Here are two exercises the author has used for many years. One shapes and controls the muscles of the pelvic girdle. The other flexes and tempers the spinal column. Practice them faithfully and you will be rewarded.

The Frog Leg Hang

Objective: To use the weight of your body to stretch and unsnarl the muscles, tendons, and ligaments of the forepart of the trunk, plus the arms and shoulders.

Position: Set up an overhead bar from which you can hang your body by lifting your feet off the ground. Or choose a rafter in the basement. Or a small horizontal tree limb. Stand on tiptoes and grasp the bar in both hands, palms facing forward. (Gloves may be needed for the tenderhanded.)

Movement: Transfer your weight gradually from your legs and feet to your hands. As you raise your feet from the ground, slowly contract the belly muscles and lift the knees toward the chest, like a frog preparing to jump. Let the body hang, your muscles stretching.

When your knees are as high as you can raise them, hold the position while counting off six seconds. Then slowly drop your feet back to the floor. Relax. Repeat three times.

Comment: This spine-straightening and abdomen-hardening technique was demonstrated to the author by Dr. John Ziegler, formerly of Olney, Maryland, and later with York, Pennsylvania, weight-training experts. It has helped many thousands. If weakened hands and arms do not permit a six-second abdominal contraction, be satisfied with whatever you can do. But do it daily at least four times a week. Soon your arms and shoulders will respond, and with them the three muscular sheaths that protect your vitals.

The Tiger Stretch

Objective: To restore the spine's elasticity, and to provide a stronger armor of muscle for the abdominal cavity and its contents.

Position: Drop down to your hands and knees, as if preparing to give a youngster a pony ride.

Movement: Bend your head toward the floor and let it hang. Hump your back as high as you can, imitating a startled cat. Holding your back high, pull up your abdominal muscles into a taut, flat sheath across the belly. Hold that position and count off six seconds. Allow the back to flatten, the abominals to sag naturally, and relax. Repeat three times. Four times each week.

Comment: Some divers have difficulty with timing their contractions while counting to ten. A useful formula uses a 2-6-2 count to cover the required ten seconds.

Count one–two for two seconds while gradually tightening your abdominals.

Count three–to–eight while holding your maximum contraction.

Count nine–ten for the final two seconds as you gradually relax.

The important thing is to find a way of getting the excercise done that works for you.

We'll say it again: A contraction of from six to ten seconds, repeated three times daily on four or more days a week, will astonish and delight you with new strength and redoubled pleasure as you continue to dive.

What about Push-Ups and Pull-Ups?

Athletic individuals from small fry to tough marines to professional footballers have all done push-ups and pull-ups ever since body conditioning was invented. If you enjoy doing them, by all means continue. Three suggestions may increase their value as conditioners.

1. Most pull-ups are performed with the palms turned to the rear. Try your next set with the palms to the front. New muscles are stimulated by this simple change, and better conditioning results.
2. Most push-ups are performed with the hands on the floor

under the shoulders. Try advancing the hands about a foot until they are opposite the *top* of your head. You will discover a whole new ballgame.

3. Try doing push-ups on your fingertips, spreading your fingers like a lion's claw pedestal under each shoulder. You can bet the excercise stimulates their muscles even more than squeezing a tennis ball.

Comment: Remember the overload principle in all the excercises you do. Just for fun, when doing pull-ups and push-ups, wear your weight belt.

5

A Perfect Dive Every Time

Conditioning drills will improve your skills, strengthen your weak points, and eliminate many of the chinks in your underwater armor. Extra muscle strength is an important factor in augmenting the enjoyment of underwater exploration.

But there is more. All unknowing, you are poised on the brink of a physical and psychic experience that comes only to the dedicated and the disciplined. Muscles can propel the sport diver into caverns and along bejeweled bottoms. If you have seen with your own eyes unbelievable submarine gardens and open water zoos, this chapter can—if you accept its challenge—introduce you to wonders that lie beneath another surface—that of your own living skin. Nature's world of water and aquatic life is a superb manifestation of the beauty and mystery of the unknown. But nature's supreme achievement, by all the measures of excellence, is still the human body and brain. Together, they await your exploration, offering even greater promises than the depths of Grand Cayman or the Great Barrier Reef.

What doorkeeper opens the portal to such wonders? Physiologists call it *endurance.*

Muscle serves one well when everything is going smoothly, but man is fallible and makes mistakes. The diver misjudges his air supply, his bottom time, the strength of a current, the distance he must swim, his ability to help a fatigued buddy to a dive boat. The list goes on.

Endurance is reserve power. It might just as well be called miracle power. Possessing it, one never panics. Using it, one evades danger.

Where does it originate?

Its well-springs are deep in the human body. Its cultivation requires only that a diver say yes to his desire to be a better human being. If he does so and follows a simple program of exercises, his reward will be a treasure greater than Spanish doubloons.

Why isn't the sport of diving sufficient to produce a fitter body? Isn't diving a physical activity? Yes, it is, but under most circumstances it lacks the catalytic ingredient called *vigor*. Vigor is what makes the pulse race and the blood tumble joyously through the heart.

"Take it easy. Breathe slow and gentle," says the divemaster.

"Give it all you've got. Drive up your heartbeat," says the master conditioner.

When things go well, an underwater expedition is a thing of joy. If things go sour, it can be a nightmare. For that reason, every diver should participate in the kind of program that will provide a reserve of endurance whenever the chips are down.

The kind of exercise program we recommend is jogging.

"What is wrong with swimming," voices cry? "Isn't it the perfect exercise?" Nothing is wrong with swimming if one really swims, if one does laps for a half-hour daily in a pool, or crawl-strokes alongside a beach for a good half-mile. What happens too often is that swimmers turn into sun bathers, more interested in tanning their skins than training their lungs. Swimming is a perfect exercise for those who will squeeze from it all the factors that produce fitness.

Jogging is preferable for two reasons. First, it permits no idling. Second, it is a year-round sport that maintains one's reserve capacity at full measure no matter what the season. Actually, it delivers a generous bonus by enabling a participant to enjoy safer diving during seasonable weather—or cross-country skiing or ice boating, not to mention ice-diving, during the winter.

Conditioning exercises come in many forms. The diver-athlete should know them all and select the one that suits him best. Let's review them briefly.

WEIGHTS

Weight training is different from weight lifting. The former utilizes weights to provide resistance to muscles so that they are stimulated to the growth which improves an athletic skill. Weight training has come to be recognized as contributing to almost any form of athletic excellence.

Weight lifting is an Olympic sport that takes the form of a contest between strong men to see who can lift the greatest poundage. These athletes develop massive muscles and great lifting power but no endurance. Their successive lifts—expressed in pounds—become higher and heavier.

Weight conditioning applies the overload principle and uses the isometric contraction of six seconds to stimulate normal muscles to greater activity. A typical exercise is the rowing movement (good for a swimmer's back, arms, and shoulders) from a horizontal trunk. To try it, bend forward at the hips and place the forehead on a desk (use a pillow). Let the arms dangle straight downward. Grasp either a fairly heavy barbell or two heavy dumbbells. Pull them slowly upward to the chest, hold for six seconds, and slowly return them to the floor. Experts recommend three series of ten repetitions each. The weight lifted should be so heavy that, after 30 lifts (3 sets x 10 reps) the exercised muscles are almost but not quite exhausted.

CIRCUIT TRAINING

Circuit training is exactly what its name implies: a circuit or loop of training stations each of which requires a different form of exercise. Equipment is necessary, so the work is usually carried on in a gymnasium. After a warm-up, the participant goes to the first station, which may be a rowing machine, then to such other activities as rope skipping, bag punching, treadmill jogging, calisthenics, weight training, beam balancing, or rope climbing. Directions are posted at each station, and a participant must keep one eye on the clock to complete his circuit within a stipulated period.

By the time he has passed through all the stations, every muscle in his body, including his heart, will have been overloaded and stimulated according to a scientific formula.

INTERVAL TRAINING

Earlier in this century, coaches and trainers discovered that the body has a "training threshhold." Specifically, unless an activity causes your heart to exceed a certain speed, you are coasting rather than training.

A Finnish physiologist named Karvonen determined that on the average the training threshhold for most humans was approximately 60 percent of their all-out capacity. Other physiologists put the level at about 160 heartbeats per minute for athletes.

Coaches quickly devised methods for hitting that training threshhold as often as possible during each afternoon's run-and-rest training period. Repeat endlessly was their formula. Interval training was the name they gave it.

The objective was to impose on muscles the greatest possible burden with the least amount of fatigue. So sprinting (getting the heartbeat high) became a part of long-distance training for running. Zatopek, the Olympian, won his first marathon after conditioning runs that included as many quarter-mile sprints as he could work into a long afternoon. The formula was and still is run hard, jog, run hard, jog, endlessly, until the light fades.

FITNESS FOR LIFE

How does one begin a program that assures fitness for life? Perhaps the easiest trail to follow is the one blazed by Bill Bowerman, celebrated track coach at Oregon University and developer of more endurance runners than any man in history. His book laid out a program embellished with times and distances.* He had just visited New Zealand and discovered an entire nation running, with middle-aged and senior citizens right up there at the leading edge of the pack. The visit changed his views about the depth of endurance. The book also laid down a solid medical background, provided by its coauthor, cardiologist W.E. Harris, of Eugene, Oregon. *Jogging* was the first jogging manual to combat the notion that age precluded activity; and when it became a best seller, the jogging boom was born.

Before Bowerman, running had meant racing to win. Suddenly, it meant fellowship and relaxation. Safety was inherent in two admonitions.

"Train, don't strain," was his first commandment.

"If you can't talk comfortably with your companion, slow down," was the second.

Bowerman and Harris promised these benefits.

Jogging improves the heart and lungs.

It makes the jogger look better and feel better.

Jogging by William Bowerman and W.E. Harris, New York: Ace Books, 1978.

He loses weight.

He reduces his waistline.

He can jog alone or in company.

He can expect to enjoy a lifetime of better health.

The list of benefits today is thrice as long because experience and research have uncovered countless new capabilities of the human machine.

THE OREGON PLAN

The Bowerman-Harris program charted the way with Plan A, for beginners of less than average fitness; Plan B, for those in average condition; and a Plan C, for persons who were better than average. Active snorkel and scuba divers are surely ready for Plan C. Here are the guidelines that led the first million joggers in America to new heights of self-enrichment.

First, the program called for a fixed schedule of three runs a week. The first two were to be executed in any way that fitted the individual's schedule. The third was to be different, an antidote to boredom. If the trainee was already a runner, Bowerman and Harris suggested a switch from cross-country to spurts, from fields to woodsy trails, from long, slow plodding to zippy intervals. Surprisingly, they asked five-day-a-week runners to cut back. Their plan prescribed a day of work, a day of rest.

Their introduction to jogging covered twelve weeks. Here are its highlights.

WEEK ONE—DISTANCE ONE MILE

Forget that you are probably fit enough to run much farther. This first week is to establish a sense of discipline, pace, and place. Soon enough, you'll be able to run free.

The ruling principle is "hard-easy." Experience with runners of all classes convinced Bowerman and Harris that even world-class runners were fatigued by a hard seven-day schedule.

Plan each week to have at least three hard days (Like Monday, Wednesday, and Friday).

Monday—Do only intervals: alternate periods of walking and jogging.

Wednesday—Slow, steady jogging or change-of-pace jogging— slow down, speed up, quick bursts.

Friday—Combine interval training with Wednesday's patterns.

How fast should one jog? The plan called for a pace of 110 yards in from fifty-five to sixty seconds.

Saturday—Take a walk, change the scenery.
Sunday—Walk and do easy stretching exercises.

For the first time, the general public was offered a program of running that did not include running to exhaustion and flatly forbade running all out. Yet it carefully husbanded the potential for physical development through the application of the principles of progression and overload. The following list of lengthening distance assignments illustrates the point.

First week — 1 mile.
Second week — 1¼ mile.
Third week — 1½ to 2 miles.
Fourth week — 1¾ to 2 miles.
Fifth week — 2 to 3 miles.
Sixth week — 2 to 3 miles.
Seventh week — 2½ to 4 miles.
Eighth week — 2¾ to 4 miles.
Ninth week — 3 to 4 miles.
Tenth week — 3½ to 5 miles.
Eleventh week — 3¾ to 5 miles.
Twelfth week — 4 to 5 miles.

The rich coaching experience of Bill Bowerman and the medical knowhow of Dr. Harris offered many helpful admonitions.

If the first week was too easy, either add to your total distance (using your own judgment) or increase the number of interval spurts and sprints.

Stretch on all your easy days.

Remember that distance assignments are permissive. Add distance as you feel the need. But never finish a workout exhausted. You should be exhilarated.

About midway through the program, you'll want to test your progress. Try jogging in the hills. If your home turf is flat, organize a Saturday or Sunday expedition to the nearest hill country. Running up a slope doubles and triples your energy loss. Run hills when you are fresh, not already tired. Finish your excursion with a long, downhill drift and you'll glow for hours.

Test your judgment of pace. Try a "jogger's mile," by setting a time-span for running it. Like eight, ten, twelve minutes. See how close you can come to running it. This is not a test of speed but of judging elapsed time. A fifteen-minute mile, by the way, can be done at a very fast walk. A seven minute mile is not a jog, it is a run. Don't forget that you are a jogger.

Look inward at yourself after about six weeks. Improvement usually comes to unfit bodies after six or seven weeks of methodical every-other-day exercise. Sometimes, the change is startling. If you were already fairly fit, you should feel improvement by your ninth or tenth week.

Keep jogging. Avoid over-training. Never go all-out. Three or four days weekly is adequate. Observe the hard-easy principle. Train, don't strain.

By today's consensus the number of times per week one should work out is four. For a long time it was three, and some physiologists still hold to that number. But runners are different, and you must reach your own decision, depending on how your body responds to your stressing it. Once you have built a reserve, you can cut back to twice a week for your maintenance program.

6

Oxygen, Carbon Dioxide, and the Human Body

The art of scuba diving produces an annual crop of needless dropouts. The causes are not hard to discover.

1. The new diver is not physically or mentally competent to withstand the stresses of underwater adventuring.
2. The new diver generally does not understand the dynamics of breathing compressed air, nor does he appreciate the rigid physical principles that can make snorkeling and scuba diving one of mankind's safest and most enjoyable hobbies.

Divers who are fit rarely drop out. Your own fitness is assured by participation in the programs outlined in Chapter 5.

So let us consider those dynamics and principles. Let us imagine that a deep breath of air—about a cupful—has reached your throat via your tank, regulator, and mouthpiece. It is ready to go to work. In scuba diving, transferring air and putting it to work in your body is the name of the game.

Technology has done all it can for you. Now, it's nature's turn, which is to say it is *your* turn. No more button pressing to move the precious stuff along. Now, your muscles and your brain have to go to work.

Air is not just nothing. You cannot see it but you can feel it—

as in a gale. What you are feeling are molecules of various kinds of gas. Roughly, four-fifths of them are nitrogen and one-fifth of them are oxygen. Air also contains traces of helium and other gases.

Let's examine your air supply's destination and the highway it must follow in your chest. You've got two lungs. The left one has two lobes, the right one three. Nobody knows why. Think of your lungs as a pair of balloons. As air enters, they expand; as it escapes, they contract. Anatomy students in med school say lungs look solid. Actually, they are sponge-like, embracing over three million tiny air sacs. Getting good air into those air sacs is what the scuba diving industry is all about.

Now we must reconnoiter the highway, or more exactly the tunnel-way, from your mouth to the air sacs in your lungs. Inhaling, you draw air through your mouth and throat until it enters the windpipe or *trachea*. A few inches below your voice-box (larynx), the windpipe divides into two smaller tubes called the *bronchi,* which connect with the right and left lungs. The route is fairly direct, but inside the lungs, it becomes a complicated maze. Here the bronchi divide and divide again into a host of tiny tunnels called *bronchioles.* The bronchioles are like a million hollow worms that penetrate every cubic inch of each lung, each bronchiole leading air to a cluster of tiny balloonlets or air sacs (like a grapevine's stem that conducts food and water to a bunch of grapes). These hollow sacs are called *alveoli.*

Where does the air go next? This is the miracle that humans share with all land creatures. The part of the air in your lungs that is oxygen—which body tissues crave—goes into your bloodstream. The walls of those millions of alveoli are so thin that certain gases can penetrate them, yet they are thick enough to contain a moving stream of blood. Because your air sacs hold a high concentration of oxygen while across the "wall" the bloodstream holds almost none, a law of physics causes the higher concentration to diffuse into the lower pressure area. Molecule by molecule, oxygen penetrates the barrier and unites with the hemoglobin in passing red corpuscles, which are immediately pushed along toward the heart.

At the same time, another transfer is happening in the opposite direction. A gas called carbon dioxide is diffusing from the blood into your alveoli. With every muscle you move, from blinking an eye to spearing a grouper, your muscle cells produce energy, heat, and waste. Waste must be eliminated. Cellular waste takes the form of lactic acid which, when the cells expel it into the bloodstream, turns into a form of body garbage called carbon dioxide. That's what you must exhale. If it stays in your system, it paralyzes the muscles. Fortunately, the blood running through your veins picks it up from all over the body and delivers it to the lungs.

Which brings us back to those thin-walled air sacs. In this reverse exchange, your blood holds a high concentration of carbon dioxide, whereas across the membrane of the air sac the air you have inhaled carries almost none. Carbon dioxide molecules, which are twenty times as active as oxygen molecules, constantly seep through the walls into the air sacs themselves.

When you exhale, the injurious carbon dioxide gas rides the air current up your windpipe and is expelled. Thus your blood is cleansed by a process that continues as long as you live. What has happened is a simple gas exchange, trading fresh oxygen for damaging carbon dioxide. It happens normally sixteen to twenty times a minute.

Remember that the function of breathing (respiration) is to bring oxygen to the lungs where your bloodstream can pick it up, to distribute it to the millions of tiny chemical factories that are your muscle cells, and then return to the lungs, carrying the waste they produce.

By means of this simple exchange of gases, you stoke uncountable furnaces as they burn the food you've eaten, after which your blood hauls aways the ashes.

PRESSURE AND THE HUMAN BODY

The human body is a poor instrument to take on a diving expedition. Its arms and legs are splendidly designed for submersion, as are its liquids. Even its skull is shaped to withstand extraordinary external stresses. Unfortunately, the rest of it is flawed by a few empty hollows, cavities, and interior tunnels that are vulnerable to the kind of pressure that produces pain.

Of itself, pressure is not bad. We live day and night under an ocean of atmosphere that exerts a tremendous pressure on each square inch of our body surfaces. The weight of a column of air one inch square reaching from sea level to the topmost molecule of the stratosphere is 14.7 pounds. Scientists designate this weight as one atmosphere—14.7 pounds per square inch (psi) at sea level.

But divers go down, not up, into an environment that is vastly different. For example, when one descends to a depth of only thirty-three feet, the extra pressure is exactly the same as that exerted by all those miles of air above. In mathematical terms, the heft of a column of water one inch square and thirty-three feet tall is 14.7 psi. Above sea level, air pressure changes so gradually that we pay almost no attention to it. Below sea level, water pressure changes with startling and sometimes dangerous rapidity.

When a diving human body submerges, its hollows and cavities are full of air at the normal surface pressure of 14.7 psi. When the body sinks to the thirty-three foot level, the pressure against its surface is the sum of the atmospheric pressure (one atmosphere) plus the pressure of thirty-three feet of water (one more atmosphere), or two atmospheres. Extrapolating this formula, at sixty-six feet the body will be under a pressure of three atmospheres, at ninety-nine feet under four atmospheres, and so on.

But inside the body, inside those hollow bony caverns of cartilage, tissue, and membrane, the pressure is still only one atmosphere—the pressure at the surface.

This difference between outside and inside pressures is diving's bane. This difference varies with depth, of course, but whatever it is, it is the source of most diving injuries.

Preventing injuries is always better than healing them. The medium that prevents injury best is compressed air. Riding in a tank on a diver's back, it is available at any depth. On command, it will flow into the mouth and throat, up the Eustacian tube to the inner ears, through the nostrils to the sinuses, and down the windpipe to the lungs. Air carries oxygen to keep the fires burning in your cells. Equally vital in diving, scuba raises the air pressure in the body's empty spaces to equal the pressure of the water overhead. Without equalization, without air pressure within the body balancing the water pressure without, one's air spaces must ultimately rupture or collapse.

Trying to equalize interior pressure during a deep dive, a skin diver can work his jaws, yawn without inhaling, or hold his nose and attempt to exhale. The scuba diver is served automatically by his regulator.

We have discussed how pressure works during descent. Let's turn to the ascent. Pressures now work in reverse. Assume that outside and inside pressures have been equalized at a considerable depth. Now the diver begins to ascend, intending to surface. As he rises, the outside pressure diminishes while at the same time the air within the lungs, sinuses, and other parts of the body begins to expand. Increasingly the diver has too much air in his lungs. They have ballooned, filling the rib cage completely, and still they seek more empty space. Somehow, this extra air must be jettisoned immediately. Unless it is "blown off," delicate membranes will rupture and leak their gases into the bloodstream, which is a prelude to serious injury.

During descent, a regulator solves a diver's pressure problems automatically. During *ascent,* he is on his own. Fortunately, a simple maneuver is available to him. He merely keeps on breathing. If this injunction seems silly, remember that man has been holding his breath under water for thousands of years. The habit is hard to break. Today, hundreds of scuba novices start an ascent instinctively holding their breath. Don't do it. The Professional Association of Diving Instructors (P.A.D.I.) says, "The most important rule in scuba diving is to breathe continuously, and never hold your breath."

If a diver continues to breathe while making a normal ascent (sixty feet or less per minute), he will blow off his surplus air and return to the surface comfortably.

Unless—there's always an "unless" in scuba diving—he has the misfortune to get a bubble trapped somewhere in his body. This bubble can be small enough to lodge beneath a filling in a tooth. Or it can be gas in the gut left over from yesterday's pork and beans. Sometimes the pain is considerable.

If it happens, says P.A.D.I., stop your ascent, wait a minute and hope the pain will subside. Continue to breathe regularly, inhaling and exhaling; and when you decide to ascend again, go upward slowly.

The prevention of injuries common to scuba diving is accomplished by observing simple rules of behavior (and using efficient diving gear). The objective is to keep internal and external pressures balanced.

Inevitably, body pressure mistakes occur resulting in injuries. Doctors call them barotraumas. *Baro* is Greek for weight, and *trauma* means injury. Divers call such accidents *squeezes.*

Squeezes—which usually happen during descent—are a consequence of a build-up of differing pressures in adjacent body structures that are separated by inadequate partitions. When a partition fails because a greater weight or pressure overcomes a lesser one, the result is any of a number of squeezes. Medical terminology names them after the body part that is squeezed or for an offending item of equipment. They are discussed hereafter, in alphabetical order as to cause, consequence, and therapy. To be safe, a scuba diver should not wait for an injury but should try to understand the natural laws by which he must abide. For this purpose, the laws of physics, as they affect the inner ear, provide an object lesson.

The ear has three chambers: the outer ear with its ear canal (for conducting sound) that ends at the eardrum; the middle ear, which begins on the inner side of the eardrum, serves as a sort of vestibule to the third and innermost compartment; and the inner ear, which houses various contraptions for hearing and maintaining balance.

In a healthy ear, the middle chamber, a damp and dark cavern, is ventilated by air that reaches it through a tiny tube discovered hundreds of years ago by an Italian named Eustachia (hence, the name *Eustacian tube*), which runs from the back of the throat to the middle ear. Sometimes, this tube becomes clogged by phlegm (during a cold), by malformation, or by swelling.

Thus it may happen that a diver submerges with a blocked Eustacian tube. When this happens, he almost immediately feels pressure and perhaps pain. Water in the ear canal has pressed against the eardrum with a pressure greater than that at the surface. Ordinarily, compressed air from the scuba tank would automatically raise the pressure in the air spaces within his skull to match the outside pressure. But when the Eustacian tube is clogged, entry of air is impossible, and the space within the inner ear remains at only one atmosphere.

So the phenomenon called the squeeze begins, the result of a greater pressure trying to enter a space of lesser pressure. Under squeeze conditions, the outside weight increases internal blood pressure and lymph pressure. When the wet tissue that lines the middle ear fills with liquids driven by the outside force, it begins to swell and its fleshy attachments to bone and cartilage strain and finally peel away. Delicate capillaries in this lining bulge with blood and weep into the central air space. If they rupture, rivulets of blood may flood the ear's interior mechanisms. Whatever happens, there is often pain so severe that it is unbearable.

Now an even greater disaster may impend. As a diver descends, the external pressure mounts and presses against an eardrum. Bending into the middle ear's empty air space, the eardrum's moorings begin to strain. If the outside pressure becomes too great, the membrane ruptures. As cold water floods the middle ear, a diver is usually disabled temporarily by an incapacitating attack of vertigo. Suddenly, he cannot walk without falling, cannot tell up from down, can neither think nor act clearly.

As the water in his ear warms to body temperature, his senses recover. During this period of disorientation, he should cling to whatever support is at hand. A ruptured eardrum provides a ready entry to bacteria and infection. As soon as lucid thought returns, a deliberate ascent is in order, followed by a visit to a physician trained to treat barotraumas.

USING COMPRESSED AIR EFFICIENTLY

The secret of using air efficiently is know-how. How does one acquire know-how before diving and how does one dive before acquiring know-how?

The basic requirement is slow, regular breathing. At all costs, whenever you dive with scuba gear, set a deliberate tempo. Practice this before diving. Use the same tempo whether you are diving with a snorkel or breathing compressed air. If you are snorkeling, puff out hard occasionally to clear your tube. Divemasters have a good reason to insist on slow breathing—it works. This is why: On the surface, your mouth and your lungs are only a dozen inches apart. Underwater, your air supply (which is carried behind your back) is separated from your mouth by two or three feet. A short breath, which works well on land, is useless here. An inhalation must be abnormally long to deliver a normal amount of oxygen. One expert explains it this way: The airways of your throat and mouth hold about a pint of air. In a short breath, you draw in about two pints, one pint for the lungs and the other pint to fill the air passages. Consider a longer breath. You can inhale as much as four pints. Assigning one pint to fill your throat and mouth, that leaves three pints for your lungs.

Realize that any extra activity consumes extra air. Some studies have shown that a scuba diver uses about one cubic foot of compressed air per minute. If he uses a seventy-gallon tank, he will be supplied (at the surface) for about seventy minutes. At thirty-three feet below (which adds another atmosphere of pressure), he will be subject to the law that doubling the pressure halves volume. Thus, his thirty-three-foot dive will exhaust his air in thirty-five minutes.

Other factors that consume energy, sometimes necessarily, are swimming against a current, towing an injured person, carrying a heavy object, or performing any labor at a hurried pace. Even using the arms to execute swimming strokes consumes energy. Try to minimize drag. Instead of walking upright on the bottom, position the body horizontally and streamline it in the direction of travel. In cold water, body heat is lost fast. Trying to maintain a comfortable temperature uses up energy, emptying an air tank with stunning speed.

Some scuba schools give students mathematical formulas for estimating their bottom time per pound of tank pressure. Many instructors discourage such calculations because they are based on averages. There's no such thing, they say, as an average diver. Each person has his own weight, his own fat padding under the skin, his own metabolic rate. These variables, they assert, throw the best estimates off.

Instead, they propose a set of basic understandings coupled with reliance on tested underwater gauges. The understandings include agreement as to who is to be the leader, who gives orders, the dive's maximum depth, and a "turn-around time" when the party agrees to start back to the dive platform. A good leader considers the experience of every member of the party and limits the dive's challenges to the least experienced. Above all, he antici- pates. For a routine dive presenting no special difficulty, a dive- master may invoke a "one-third" rule. When his air gauge shows that only one-third of his air is unused, he leads the way home with the assurance that his party has enough air remaining to handle chance accidents. In cave diving or other difficult expedi- tions, the leader may demand even stricter control by invoking the one-half rule. When his air is half-gone, he signals, "Let's get out of here."

7

Diving Maladies

Millions of men and women have breathed compressed air during the last quarter-century with remarkably few injuries. Our best statistics (though they are incomplete) indicate that the sport of scuba diving becomes progressively safer each year as divers and doctors become more familiar with its vagaries.

To date, most of the maladies afflicting scuba buffs originate either in carelessness or in a lack of comprehension of the laws of physics. The gases in the air we breathe on the surface often display a different kind of behavior a few fathoms down.

Fortunately, most of the diving gremlins have been tamed.

This chapter contains a list of some of the maladies that still stage an occasional raid on diving parties. Invariably, they choose to harass the careless and uninformed. Although we cannot control a diver's carelessness, we can hope to improve his knowledge.

Most divers will never experience the majority of the maladies described. Good divers, however, should know about them, understand them, and be prepared to assist in controlling them.

AIR EMBOLISM

Air embolism is a strange malady in which compressed air escapes from the air sacs of the lungs and invades the bloodstream and body spaces from within the chest, causing all sorts of pain and other mischief. As usual, pressure is the villain.

To repeat the familiar story, a descending scuba diver's lungs fill with air so that internal pressure matches that of the outside water. As a diver ascends, the outside water pressure diminishes, leaving excess pressure within the lungs. As he continues his ascent, the outside pressure diminishes even more, whereas the air pressure in the lungs remains the same, becoming increasingly excessive. In this situation, the compressed air inside the lungs expands until they fill the chest cavity and beyond. If a diver does not realize what is happening, something unpleasant occurs.

Hundreds (perhaps thousands) of air sacs or alveoli in the lungs, under pressure from within, swell, tear, and burst. Streams of air bubbles flow into the bloodstream and into whatever air spaces they can penetrate. (See entries on pneumo-thorax, mediastinal emphysema, and skin squeeze.)

Bubbles entering the blood are carried quickly to the heart which pumps them into the body's general circulation. Because bubbles are light, many rise toward the head threatening potential strokes. Wherever they go, they sweep along, traversing arteries, arterioles, and capillaries until some of them become jammed in tunnels too tiny for their passage. Like miniature plugs, they dam the flow, stopping circulation. Cells located downstream from the blockage cannot live long with their oxygen and nutrients cut off. Soon they begin to dry up and die.

A careless diver rising to the surface may not know what is happening to him. He may climb onto the dive platform well pleased with himself. Symptoms usually show up within a few minutes. They can be blurred vision, breath shortage, partial paralysis, or a bloody foam on the lips. Sometimes there's pain in the chest as if from a violent blow. Convulsions may follow.

Treatment

Survival of a severe attack of air embolism depends on eliminating the bubbles in the victim's blood. Only a recompression chamber can do this properly. As in decompression sickness, the victim should be *rushed* to the nearest naval or hospital recompression facility. During transportation, the victim should be laid on his left side with legs and feet elevated 20 to 30 degrees to prevent additional bubbles from reaching the brain. A tilt board improvised from a plank is helpful. Apply artificial respiration for as long as there are vital signs. Again, the ultimate treatment is recompression.

Prevention

Prevention begins at the start of a diver's ascent. Air embolism can happen in as few as ten feet of water. The diver must breathe normally all the way to the surface, never holding his breath, and maintaining a rate of ascent slightly slower than that of his bubbles, or about sixty feet per minute. To repeat, every good instructor insists strongly on *never, never* holding one's breath while ascending.

Note: Air embolism and decompression sickness are deceptively similar. Both are the result of too much gas in the blood and body cells. But they are different in these respects:

Air embolism is caused by compressed air.

Decompression sickness is caused by nitrogen.

Air embolism occurs when the walls of air sacs rupture and air bubbles enter the blood and body.

Decompression sickness occurs when the nitrogen portion of one's compressed air is inhaled, absorbed into the blood stream through lung membranes, and then forms nitrogen bubbles.

Many symptoms fit either malady.

CARBON DIOXIDE POISONING

Carbon dioxide (CO_2) is the gaseous form of your body's cellular debris. It forms when your cells burn the food your blood has delivered. It is synthesized in the tissues and excreted through the lungs. If each cell in the body is considered a tiny furnace, CO_2 might be called the smoke. A healthy body gets rid of it quickly. Plants inhale it greedily and release oxygen, which is part of nature's grand recycling design.

Under water, CO_2 is a menace, especially to scuba beginners. Actually, modern open-end scuba gear has almost eliminated its threat. Closed-end gear (where your exhaust breath goes into a charcoal "cleaner" supposed to absorb the CO_2) is a greater hazard. We discuss it here because your understanding of what happens might save a life.

When the air you inhale reaches a level of about 3 percent CO_2, you're at the edge of your usual tolerance. From 3 to 6 percent, you will feel distress. If the level rises to 10 percent, you will probably black out.

Where does this carbon dioxide come from? As already explained, it originates in the cells as a waste product and rides the bloodstream into the lungs, where it filters through the membrane of your alveoli or air sacs, thence into your windpipe from which it is expelled. Topside, CO_2 is exhaled into the atmosphere where it dissipates harmlessly. Under water, if you use a two-hose regulator, you breathe it into a rubber tube.

Some divers, especially the inexperienced, become so anxious about their next breath that they do not exhale hard enough to flush away all this waste gas. Instead, a small amount remains in the tube to be sucked back into the lungs with the next inhalation and added to the next expiration. Thus, the CO_2 level rises.

Use a modern regulator and avoid trouble. Waste gas goes through the mouthpiece's ports and directly into the water where it forms bubbles that rise to the surface.

Prevention

How does one avoid CO_2 poisoning?

Concentrate on regular, rhythmic, deep exhalations. Don't breathe jerkily, don't skip-breath (holding every other breath). With each breath, empty your lungs comfortably. It's easy, but you must work at it consciously until it becomes a habit.

Check yourself for fatigue. Be suspicious if you've felt great but suddenly in the midst of a dive feel washed-out. Some divers have felt such an overwhelming sense of depression or exhaustion that they have lain down on the bottom of the ocean and died.

Check your face plate; is it fogged? Cold water can cause a fog, but so does CO_2 in your breath. If you suspect you're being poisoned, flush the lungs with deep exhalations. If possible, pacify the mind and body and hold on to something. Signal to your buddy that you suspect trouble. He'll probably offer you air from his tank. Take it; your own air might be contaminated.

Symptoms may not hit until after you have surfaced and sat a while. If you hear a companion say your eyes are rolling, if you are acting silly, tipsy, dizzy, or threatening to pass out or if your lips are blue, your problem is probably CO_2 poisoning. Break out your oxygen bottle (you should carry one) and take some straight. If fresh air alone is available, see that it comes from the windward side of any nearby gas engine exhaust. And wait.

CARBON MONOXIDE POISONING

Carbon monoxide (CO) is the stuff that comes from the exhausts of automobile engines and kills people. If you breathe enough of it, accidentally or otherwise, you've had it. It forms when a carbon compound is burned without adequate oxygen. How can an underwater diver get carbon monoxide in his lungs? It's easy.

Most air compressors are run by gasoline engines. Their

exhausts emit carbon monoxide, which is without color or taste and is very poisonous. Its molecules are fantastically active. Given a chance, they combine with the hemoglobin in the blood at a rate two-hundred times faster than oxygen. They form a compound called carboxyhemoglobin. When red cells (hemoglobin) are loaded with carboxyhemoglobin, there's no place left for the oxygen molecules that keep the body alive. The blood rushes uselessly around accomplishing nothing and leaving a trail of oxygen-starved cells. If cells starve long enough (minutes will do it), they die.

How does CO get into your air tank? It gets there *(1)* when an ill wind blows some of a gas engine's exhaust into the air compressor's intake; or *(2)* when the oil that lubricates a compressor's cylinders becomes super-hot and "flashes" (fails to burn totally) or "diesels." Therefore, it is imperative that a diver purchase scuba tank air refills only from an experienced and reliable dealer, dive shop operator, or dive boat master.

At surface pressure, most people can breathe a little carbon monoxide without penalty—and do so in every traffic jam. At thirty-three feet under the surface, the poison's pressure is doubled, at sixty-six feet it is tripled, and so on. Thus, at depth blood soaks up what was only a harmless trace topside and makes it lethal.

Symptoms include headache, giddiness, ringing in the ears, vomiting, vertigo, loss of memory, fainting, collapse, paralysis, unconsciousness, and changes in the heart's rhythm. Visible signs are skin that may be flushed or bluish or (less often) a cherry pink face and lips. Another sign is a failure of muscular coordination. Unconsciousness often hits before one is aware that something is amiss.

Treatment

Loosen clothing and keep the victim warm. If he is unconscious, give artificial respiration for at least one hour. Call for a doctor, preferably an aqua-doctor. If it is available, give 100 percent oxygen for up to ninety minutes. Pure oxygen is said to clear carbon monoxide from hemoglobin in from thirty to ninety minutes. Plain fresh air takes longer—two hours or more. Experienced aqua-doctors agree that a coma that persists beyond these time limits has probably damaged the brain beyond repair.

Prevention

Again, deal only with reputable suppliers. If you are a stranger to a diving area, ask local divers where they buy their air. Or test your air purchases for carbon monoxide and oil vapor yourself. Pocket-size testing kits are available at dive shops. They are especially useful to divers who patronize out-of-the-way dive sites. Finally, at the slightest whiff of impure air, call off your dive and investigate.

DECOMPRESSION SICKNESS (THE BENDS)

Decompression sickness, often called the *bends,* is not a disease like influenza or measles caused by germs. It is a condition that changes the composition of countless cells in your body. That condition can come about when a diver breathes so much compressed air that his body absorbs an excessive amount of nitrogen.

Air, you recall, is composed roughly of one-fifth oxygen and four-fifths nitrogen. Compressed air carries the same proportion, and when its hyped-up molecules hit your lungs, they dive into your bloodstream. Your circulation then distributes them wherever blood flows. If your dive is short, your absorption is inconsequential. If your dive is lengthy, your load of nitrogen becomes a time bomb. The length of your stay under water determines the degree of your saturation.

As you rise toward the surface, external water pressure drops. The inside air pressure, however, can diminish only as fast as the excess gases in your body are exhaled. This is a slow process, so slow that supersaturated tissues begin to act like an uncapped bottle of fizz water. Bubbles form and try to escape from the bloodstream as it passes through the lungs. A few make it, but most don't; and these bubbles roll on through the heart and into your arteries which get smaller and smaller. Finally they get into such tight quarters that they become wedged in place, blocking the blood flow. In the brain, that blockage can cause a stroke. In the heart, a coronary. In the spine, paralysis. But first there is awful pain, usually in the joints of the arms and legs. It is called the bends.

Remember that a normal amount of nitrogen in the system is no problem. Even a pressure of two atmospheres seems tolerable. More than that is bad news. More than that is what you may get if you dive too deep.

Fortunately, the United States Navy has learned how to eliminate too much nitrogen. A diver needs merely to ascend slowly—very slowly—stopping at times to allow that surplus nitrogen to bubble out through his mouth. Instructions are simple, based on thousands of Navy tests. If you stay down for so many minutes, then you must take so many more minutes to make your ascent. This repeated rise-and-wait process is called decompression. Follow the figures in the Navy's decompression tables, and you'll get home okay. Take a short-cut, and you'll probably get decompression sickness.

Long, deep dives, those over one-hundred feet, are always an adventure, but they become dangerous when the diver disregards his tables, dives with a bad cold or a hangover, expends too much energy, dives while physically unfit or over-fat, or plunges into water that absorbs too much of his body heat.

Some attacks of the bends hit a victim under water, some on the surface. Many divers feel fine on surfacing and then—usually within thirty minutes—experience symptoms.

One warning is a localized pain in arm, elbow, or knee. It starts as a slight ache and then flares to unbearable agony. Beware of an itchy skin, numbness, or a tingling sensation. Skin rash often ensues, with mottling and blotching. In rare cases, the victim has difficulty breathing, chokes, and shows signs of paralysis. These are indications of a serious attack.

Treatment

No medication can cure an attack of the bends. The only known prompt cure is a period spent in a recompression chamber. Such equipment is available at certain naval installations and at many hospitals. Dive shops and diving instructors know where they are. Before making a dive, have the address and phone number of the nearest chamber in your gear, ready for emergency use.

Some early books on scuba diving suggest that a victim of the bends can be decompressed by taking him into the water and down to a level of 165 feet and then bringing him up slowly, belatedly following the correct Navy table. Not so, say today's authorities. The victim can lose consciousness under water, altogether a bad scene. In addition, two extra divers would be needed. Don't try it. By any means possible, get the victim into a recompression tank as fast as possible, even though it is hours away. Law enforcement agencies usually know where to go and are eager to help. If you fly, stay at low altitude. The higher you fly, the more nitrogen will bubble out of the victim's tissues, making the bends worse.

Signs of severe bends are a weak and fast pulse, cold and clammy extremities, dilated pupils, bluish lips and nails, shallow breathing, even nausea. Place the patient on his back, with legs elevated. Turn the head to one side to prevent choking. Warm his body with blankets or rugs. Unless there is excessive vomiting, small sips of water are permissable. No alcohol! Rubbing the hands and feet toward the heart helps move blood. Do all this while waiting for transportation or while en route to a hospital and professional assistance. Feed the victim pure oxygen, if any is available. An unconscious victim presents special problems. Is his heart strong? Are his chest muscles working? Watch his pulse and respiration. If he needs help, use mouth-to-mouth resuscitation.

In a nutshell, no emergency is likely to occur if a diver ascends according to those carefully plotted Navy dive tables, and if he pauses at each level until his watch tells him to move up to the next step. Every minute of the return ascent from a deep dive must be planned *before* the dive. Those pauses give his cells time to eliminate their superfluous nitrogen. Respect them, and all should be well.

In fact, no sport diver should ever get himself into such a fix, according to the Professional Association of Diving Instructors. "Decompression diving is beyond the scope of recreational diving," they assert. "Sport divers should always dive within established decompression limits on *all* dives."

EMERGENCY ASCENT

"His particular emergency ascent consisted of a quick flip of his weight belt buckle, a pull at the carbon-dioxide cartridge cord dangling from his life vest, and swimming motions to the surface. His actions took only fractions of a second, and they saved his life." That's Mort Walker writing about a diver in his book, *Sport Diving.**

At eightly feet, the friend had been confronted by the worst of deep water emergencies; he lost his air tank. Somehow, it slipped from its harness, jerked the mouthpiece from his jaws, and disappeared. His lungs were almost empty. Instinct told him that the only way out was up. Good training prescribed his mental reaction.

Dropping his weight belt, he began to rise. Too slow. Popping his BDC added lift that increased as it expanded. Flipper kicks and arm strokes built up his speed. Exhaling all the way, he burst through the surface like a porpoise.

He had saved his life by breaking the safety-first rule against a fast ascent, taking his chance of being crippled by the "bends,"

*Sport Diving: The Instructional Guide to Skin & Scuba, Chicago: Contemporary Books, 1977.

nitrogen poisoning, or air embolism. Under such circumstances, racing to a compression chamber was a pleasant option.

Happily, he won. He won for two reasons: he did all the right things, and he was lucky. Whoever dives with scuba gear always runs the chance of having to make an emergency ascent. From day one, he must be aware of that fact, and of what he can do about it. Here are helpful suggestions refined from the experiences of many divers.

1. Keep cool. Spend a few seconds reviewing your situation. Find your buddy. Determine your depth. Think of your options.
2. Decide whether to swim for it or ask your buddy for help. With your BCD working, you can rise faster than you can move horizontally. If your buddy and the surface are the same distance away, head for the surface. If your buddy is close at hand, ask for buddy breathing.
3. Once you've started buddy breathing and are making a joint ascent, stick together. Records show that a distressed diver who abandons his buddy on the way to the surface is apt to be severely injured.
4. Never abandon your own air supply or your own regulator even though no air is flowing at the moment. As you rise, expansion within your cylinder usually makes some of your own air available. It is also useful to realize that recent studies have shown that it is more hazardous to exhale continuously during a rapid ascent than to interrupt your exhalation with attempts at inhalation. This latest scientific "poop," not yet generally known hints that the old "Blow and go" motto is the wrong way to make a *fast* ascent.
5. Probably your greatest danger from an emergency ascent is lung overexpansion. The faster you go, the faster your lungs expand, which can be dangerous. Sure, you'll be in a hurry, but don't take off like a pickerel. If you were a jogger, you might increase your speed to a mild gallop. But you're a diver, so pace yourself halfway between a slow breast stroke and a Mark Spitz sprint. Easy does it.
6. If you're 100 feet under and your gauge shows absolute zero air, hold yourself together long enough to begin a *normal* ascent. Escaping from that situation may be an emergency, right! But your ascent to the top certainly is not. Here's why! There is still a little good air in your tank. Outside pressure has shut it off temporarily, but as you rise it will expand,

providing enough of that sweet stuff to get you all the way to the surface. Knowing that fact is a comforting feeling when every nerve end is yelling "May Day!"

HOOD SQUEEZE

Hood squeeze affects the outer ear canal. If your dive suit hood covers both ears and seals out water, trouble is almost certain. With a watertight hood, you will be diving with your outer ears empty except for air at sea-level pressure. Thirty-three feet down, the water pressure will double. Drop another thirty-three feet, and the pressure will triple. The effect of this is to create a partial vacuum between your outer ears and your hood; and the outer faces of your eardrums must pay the price.

If the pressure differential across the ear lining is moderate, you may escape with no greater damage than a constellation of blood blisters in the canal. If a blister bursts, there may be bleeding. If the differential becomes insupportable, then the eardrum, pushed hard by the compressed air fed into your middle ear can burst *outward*.

Prevention

Make certain that your hood does not entirely block water from your ears. Some divers line their hoods with foam rubber pads, one over each ear. This provides space to admit water without sacrificing protection and warmth.

Another method—useful under water—is to pick up a small fold of your hood between your thumb and finger, lift both hood and the edge of your mask where they overlap, and exhale through your nostrils. This permits pressurized air from your lungs to flow through the mask into the area about your ears, balancing the inner and outer pressures. As you descend, continue this maneuver, equalizing as you go. Next dive, make certain your ears have direct access to the outside water.

If you wear a bathing cap instead of a hood, use pads of sponge to permit water to reach your ear canals as above, or else tuck up the cap's border so that it rides *above* the ears. In diving, the passage to the eardrum must be kept open to water. For the same reason, never use ear plugs.

INTERSTITIAL EMPHYSEMA SQUEEZE

The dictionary describes emphysema as the presence of air in lung tissue *between* the alveoli caused by a rupture of these alveoli. When air makes its way into the interstices of this tissue, the result is the malady called interstitial emphysema. Like so many others, it is a consequence of excessive pressure that a diver failed to equalize.

If damage is done to the lung capillaries, some of this interstitial air is likely to slip into the bloodstream, forming bubbles. If the damage occurs under many feet of water, those bubbles will expand during ascent and lodge—possibly in an artery or vein, compromising your circulation.

The only treatment is decompression.

Prevention

The rupture of alveoli within a diver's lungs usually takes place when he neglects to breathe normally or rises too fast during his ascent to the surface.

LUNG SQUEEZE (SPONTANEOUS PNEUMOTHORAX)

Each of your lungs is wrapped in a snug, glistening sack of air-tight membrane called the pleura. The two lungs are located atop the diaphragm and contained in a larger sack of the same material that forms the inner lining of the pleural cavity or thorax—which most people call the rib cage.

Ordinarily, not a single bubble of air is to be found in the space between the lung coverings and the rib cage lining. These inner sacks move against the outer lining, rising and falling in rhythm with the movement of the ribs. Moisture-lubricated, frictionless, smooth as mother-of-pearl, the membranes usually last a lifetime.

Under certain conditions, because of a diver's ignorance or carelessness, the chest space is invaded by air, which causes a malady or squeeze called spontaneous pneumothorax. It happens when the sack surrounding one of the lungs is ruptured and the air within (plus some occasional fleshy debris) is blown into the rib cage.

It can happen during a rapid emergency ascent or a deep dive. Whether the injury comes from the inside or outside of the body, this creates a passageway for air from the inner lung to enter the sealed-off rib cage, and the condition is serious! The lung begins to collapse like a punctured balloon. Since a lung rupture occurs only at a level considerably below the surface, that air is always highly pressurized. As the injured diver ascends, the air trapped in the chest space may expand to twice or three times its sea-level volume. This expansion collapses the lung into itself and puts half of one's breathing apparatus out of action. It also introduces the possibility of dangerous infection.

Treatment

See a physician fast! This rule applies to all chest squeezes in which air is trapped within the thoracic cavity—mediastinal emphysema, subcutaneous emphysema, and general lung squeeze.

Prevention

Obey all the common-sense rules formulated and taught by every responsible diving instructor, such as "Never hold your breath when ascending. Never pass your bubbles going up. Never exceed your bottom time in the no-compression Naval table. Never try to break a depth record." Remember, the accepted rule of thumb for sport diving is to limit one's depth to one-hundred feet.

MASK SQUEEZE

You have surfaced and taken off your face mask, and your dive buddy is looking at you intently. Coming closer, he peers into your eyes, touches your face. When you wipe your nose, you see blood. Thinking back, you recall the first pain behind your eyes, but it passed and you continued your dive. You've just experienced a mask squeeze. It could have been worse.

How does it happen? The air within your face mask constitutes a small bubble outside of but attached to your body. It becomes dangerous when its sea-level pressure becomes considerably lower than the pressure built-up within your sinuses and nasal airways. If this disparity increases too much, the internal air, following nature's law, tries to invade the area of lower pressure in the mask. The most direct route is through the eyes and skin. At the same time, you feel the pressure of the mask against your face as the outside water pressure exerts itself against the air bubble beneath the faceplate. As a result, your facial tissues are squeezed.

Treatment

First aid for a slight squeeze is a cold compress (ice water if available) applied as soon as possible and changed every ten minutes. Next day, use hot compresses. For anything worse or if the pain does not go away or if bleeding from the nose persists, consult a doctor as soon as you can after leaving the water.

Prevention

You have an airway from your lungs into your face mask through your nose. If you ever feel pain behind the eyes, exhale through it. Divers become so accustomed to inhaling and exhaling through their mouthpieces that they rarely breathe through the nose. Mask squeeze can be prevented only by building up the air pressure inside the mask to equal that of the internal air space. So exhale slowly into the mask while pressing its rim gently against your face to create a perfect seal. Never inhale through the nose—that reduces the pressure.

MEDIASTINAL EMPHYSEMA OR SUBCUTANEOUS EMPHYSEMA SQUEEZE

Loose bubbles in the chest, once they have escaped from the lung's air sacs, can lodge in the mediastinum, a crowded space within the upper chest that includes all the central area not already filled by the lungs themselves. Mostly, it is the space between the two lung structures housing the heart, aorta, vena cava, other blood vessels, various nerves, and tissue.

Symptoms are severe pain under the breastbone radiating into the shoulders and arms. Shortness of breath results when air in the chest expands and presses against respiratory passages. Swallowing may become difficult. Breathing may be labored.

Some bubbles frequently climb to the base of the neck, rumpling the surface of the skin. This phenomenon is both visible and audible. The skin puffs up from the air beneath it. When it is rubbed, it crackles. Talking, swallowing, and breathing become an effort, and the voice changes. This condition is called subcutaneous emphsema or neck squeeze. Alone, it seldom causes great trouble, but because it usually accompanies mediastinal emphysema, it should be taken seriously.

Treatment

First aid is not enough. Recompression is the usual practice.

MIDDLE EAR SQEEZE

Middle ear squeeze happens when the ear's middle chamber is sealed off from the compressed air supply by a blocked Eustacian tube. Usually, it hurts a lot. This malady accounts for about half of all medical problems caused by diving.

Your ear starts to ache almost immediately after you submerge. Something is unmistakably wrong, but you argue to yourself that you are barely beneath the surface. Ear squeeze happens often at about ten feet. You continue to descend, unwilling to give up. You've heard that some divers make a practice of "diving through" their pain. It usually doesn't work, and it can be dangerous.

For some, the pain increases, for some it decreases. It may be replaced by a ringing in the ears, or buzzes, clicks, and roars. If you continue, you may feel a sudden, retching sensation and the swirling disorientation of instant vertigo. It happens when an eardrum bursts and cold water pours into the inner ear.

In case of such an attack, grab a line or rock or whatever is handy and hang on. Your sense of direction may evaporate temporarily, leaving no sense of up, down, or sideways. It takes a minute or two for the water in your ear to warm to body temperature, and for your recovery. Find your dive buddy. More than likely, he has already responded to your drunken actions. Let him take charge and help you back to the surface.

You can never dive free and easy unless your Eustacian tubes are open. As you leave the surface, your body spaces contain air at surface pressure. As you descend, the water pressure increases, and this force is transmitted through your body to your hollow inner spaces.

In the middle ear, this outer pressure impinges on its walls, linings and blood vessels. With clear Eustacian tubes, your breathing brings an abundance of compressed air into the middle ear. With blocked tubes, each foot of descent increases your jeopardy.

A squeeze develops by stages. Blood vessels swell and bulge. Blood oozes into the ear's lining. Presently, the vessels break, flooding the swollen tissue. If the process continues, the lining swells and peels away from its bony support. At the same time, water pressure against the outside of the eardrum forces it inward. Finally, its fragile, damaged fabric tears and it is swept aside by the in-rush of water.

Clearing the Eustacian tubes by popping the ears is the first task of every careful sport diver after submersion. Traditional methods include waggling the jaw from side to side, swallowing, or blowing forcefully (but not too hard) against pinched nostrils. If these efforts fail, ascend several feet and try again. Do not descend until your Eustacian tubes are open and your ears are clear.

Anticongestants have been touted as a happy solution for divers whose ears are blocked by a bad cold. Maybe! Many dive shops carry these drugs. Allegedly, they reduce swelling and congestion.

Favorites for predive use include Schering's Afrin and Burroughs-Welcome's Sudafed. It is suggested that such products be used only after medical approval.

Warnings

If you feel ear pain during a dive and you continue to descend, a ruptured ear drum will probably result.

A scuba beginner who wants to know if he can clear his Eustacian tubes can sometimes find out by skin diving to the bottom of a swimming pool. Holding his breath, and hanging onto a ladder's bottom or a weight to stay under water, he should pop his ears by swallowing hard, waggling his jaw, or using one of the other tricks described above. If his tubes clear readily, he can feel the difference. It not, he should get professional advice on the advisability of continuing to dive.

If you have frequent colds, asthma, a perforated eardrum, frequent external ear infections, chronic hay fever, or a record of mastoid operations, you are probably disqualified as a sport diver.

If your head feels uncomfortable following a dive, consult an ear, nose, and throat physician. If you do burst an eardrum, it's not the end of the world. If there are no complications, healing usually takes two or three weeks. A small tear might heal in a few days. Usually, there is no loss of hearing.

Remember that fresh blood in an ear offers an inviting home for bacteria. Don't mess with it. Germs ride in on swabs, fingers, handkerchiefs, etc. If you suspect a ruptured eardrum, tape a bandage across your ear and consult a physician.

REPETITIVE DIVING

Novice divers, like skiers, enjoy their fun so much that they want to repeat it over and over. Repeating underwater forays within the same 12-hour diving day can lead to disaster. Every dive that uses scuba equipment leaves a residue of nitrogen in the body. At the surface, a diver usually "blows off" this excess with ordinary breathing, but complete elimination takes at least 12 hours. Each dive in a series performed *on the same day* is bound to leave some nitrogen residue since intermissions are never long enough to eliminate the gas accumulation. In itself, this surplus does no harm. As it builds, however, it can throw a diver into decompression sickness unless he plans his depth and bottom times as guided by Navy tables. If you dive with a divemaster, and if you want to dive more than once on the same day, ask him to monitor your excursions. If an expert is not available, turn yourself into one by studying the subject, mastering the Navy no-compression tables, and calculating your procedures carefully before challenging the build-up in your body of nitrogen.

SINUS SQUEEZE

Sinuses are small cavities in your skull that open into the air compartments of the nose. Eight in number, they are paired so that four lie on each side of the face. Actually, they are merely odd-shaped empty caves with walls of thin bone covered with the same membrane as the nose and throat.

Secretions from the sinuses drain by gravity through tiny tunnels into the nasal structure. If any one of a diver's eight passages becomes clogged, it can cause a painful squeeze.

The situation is basically the same as that of the middle ear. If the air in a sinus is sealed off by swollen tissue, under diving conditions it may act as a vacuum and cause considerable pain or discomfort. As long as the tunnels stay open, no complications should arise. Ordinarily, sinuses are free of germs. But a head cold can quickly fill them with mucus and misery.

The mechanism of a sinus squeeze is this: The air in a diver's sinus is sealed off when its drainway becomes plugged. Air pressure within it remains at one atmosphere (surface pressure). When he dives, the water pressure on his body increases and this pressure is transmitted through his skull to the sealed-off sinus wall and lining. As a pressure differential builds up, the lining fills with extruded blood and begins to ooze. The result is pain, inflammation, and possible infection. Under such circumstances, all diving is forbidden.

Symptoms: The frontal sinus is typical and lies across the forehead above the eyes and on both sides of the nose. Divers gripe about it frequently. If you cannot get compressed air into this sinus during a dive, a sharp, stabbing pain will strike the region of the eyebrows. With a prompt return to the surface, the pain will vanish. Sometimes the entire face aches with pain concentrated behind the nose. You might taste blood or see blood drops on the inside of your faceplate. This is not necessarily bad; you may have ruptured only a small blood vessel in the nasal passage. If there is a *flow* of blood surface immediately, and take it as a warning that you should consult a physician.

Treatment

You may have incurred a case of sinusitis. Most such infections clear up in about three weeks. Nose drops may help you sleep comfortably. Some patients react quickly to vasoconstrictor drugs, pills, or capsules, taken orally. Ask your druggist for suggestions. Don't dive again until your doctor gives you his permission.

8

Topside Hazards

For many reasons, treating one's own injury is "in."

In many areas, physicians are in short supply. Or they are specialists with little knowledge of athletic or diving disabilities. Or their fees have rocketed beyond the average diver's capacity to pay.

Taking care of yourself (and your buddy) always saves time. Under some circumstances, it can save a life. Hundreds of thousands of Americans have learned the Heimlich maneuver and cardio-pulmonary resuscitation (CPR). Today, the stranger who pops out of a crowd to offer first aid is rarely a doctor. Usually, he is a card-carrying, certified Good Samaritan. And there's a bonus. Being your own doctor sometimes is fun.

The do-it-yourself therapist attending the victim of an auto accident or of a scuba mishap needs to know only a few basic procedures. He or she must

Know how to identify and appraise an injury.

Know how to stop bleeding.

Know the proper use of cold and heat in treating injuries.

Know how to prevent and control infection.

Know how to perform the Heimlich maneuver.

Be able to do external heart massage and mouth-to-mouth breathing (CPR).

Recognize the conditions under which professional medical assistance is necessary.

Not all the crises in a sport diver's life take place below the water's surface or even at a dive resort. Like less specialized hobbyists, he must travel by bus, van, or car. He must sometimes tramp into remote forests to reach a secluded spring or cave. He endures bites on land and in the water and abrasions above and below the surf, and he suffers from motion sickness and jet lag exactly like other mortals.

This chapter contains information about a wide range of possible injuries and ailments. It is intended to complement your own first-hand experience. In brief but inclusive entries, it represents the thinking of the established medical community. It should add to the depth and breadth of knowledge by which sport divers can ameliorate suffering.

ABRASIONS (SKIN BURNS AND SCRAPES)

Abrasions come in many sizes but in only two depths—shallow and deep. Shallow abrasions can be handled at home or in the field. Deep abrasions, which penetrate the skin and reach into the muscle tissue, require a physician's attention.

Abrasions can happen in the open or under water. One can get a bad scrape from handling heavy gear, boats, tanks, or from almost any activity. Under water, one may scrape against barnacle-encrusted pilings, timbers, or rusted metals. Coral reefs and rocky subterranean passages are also a hazard (long underwear offers some protection). Frequently, the diver will be unaware of an unjury because cold water has a numbing effect.

Treatment involves five steps: washing, cleansing, medicating, bandaging, and fighting infection.

Washing

Friction has scraped away a section of the top layer of skin, often leaving a multitude of bleeding points through which an army of germs can march. Counterattack at once by washing with soap and water. If the soap is germicidal, so much the better. Washing a deep abrasion can hurt. Cool, running water eases the pain. One divemaster we know first rubs a wound gently with a wet bar of soap, sweeping off ground-in rust specks, shell particles, rock dust splinters, or whatever. If a vegetable spray is at hand, its jet may be useful. The objective is to remove every bit of foreign matter. A bath of hydrogen peroxide will sometimes dislodge embedded particles.

If the wound is too deep to clean yourself, call a doctor. If its bottom doesn't have a skin-like appearance, call a doctor. If the pain is too great for you to do a thorough job, call a doctor. He will probably use a pain-killing anesthetic and give you a shot to kill germs. If your tetanus shot has run out, he'll probably give you a booster.

After the abrasion is thoroughly washed, go after any remaining debris embedded in your skin with a sterile needle or pair of tweezers. Using a magnifying glass in proper surrounding light helps to find minuscule particles.

Often, your abrasion may present a loose flap of skin. If it is clean, leave it alone and press it back in place gently to act as a natural dressing. If it's dirty, cut it off with fingernail scissors.

Treatment

Most of today's healers refuse to irritate the skin with such old standbys as iodine, mercurochrome, or raw alcohol. They claim those treatments did more harm than good. Some medics advise skipping any kind of antiseptic in order to go directly to an antibiotic ointment. Dr. Gabe Mirkin, a famous sports physician, recommends Mycitracin, Neo-Polycin, Neosporin, or Polysporin, all obtainable without prescription at a drugstore.

Wartime experience has demonstrated that an unbandaged wound usually heals faster than one that is covered. A tight dressing keeps a wound moist and thus promotes unwanted bacterial growth. If possible, don't cover an abrasion. However, if clothing rubs against it, protection must be provided. Here a light gauze pad smeared with a thin coating of antibiotic ointment is in order. Remove the dressing each night. Exposing the wound to the air will dry it out. If the bandage sticks, soften it with a bath of hydrogen peroxide by soaking it until it slips off easily.

There is available a good nonsticking bandage material called Telfa. Placing it over the wound and using adhesive tape to hold it in place provides protection against irritation and contamination from trouser legs, skirts, or shirt sleeves. If the scrape is under a sock or beltline, definitely use a Telfa pad. When a dressing gets wet or becomes dirty, clean and dress the wound every day. Remember that healing takes place from the inside out.

Your major responsibility is to prevent infection. Nature has distributed tetanus spores all over the earth, even in its waterways and oceans. They are lying in wait. Most abrasions clear up without complications. Healing time is shorter for young people than for seniors, but it varies widely within the same age group. So even while expecting an early recovery, watch for danger signs.

Infection turns a wound an angry red and makes it feel hot. The greater the infection, the worse the pain. Pus develops and drains away. Lymph glands swell and hurt in your groin, neck, or armpits. Red streaks may radiate outward from the wound. The body temperature rises.

One or more of these signs indicates that you might be heading for trouble. The moment you suspect an abrasion is infected, call a doctor and describe your symptoms. If you cannot reach him, soak the wound in hot salt water four times each day, and follow each soaking with an application of antibiotic ointment. If you are at sea, head for port.

ALCOHOL

Don't let the paeans of praise bestowed on beer in *Runners World* magazine persuade you that a sport diver can improve his performance by diving with a six-pack. The authors of the article were speaking to long-distance runners when they described Dr. Tom Bassler's habit of drinking a pint of beer every five miles, and they were pointing out that long-distance racing dehydrates the body. Diving doesn't. They were saying that excessive sweating drains off much-needed potassium. Diving doesn't. They were really telling runners to drink plenty of liquids (of any kind), and that beer contains useful amounts of potassium. They were saying that muscle cells can become too dry to function during a marathon race. But not in a dive.

Alcohol attacks the central nervous system. Very small amounts might improve skilled performance in some people, but imbibing only a few drops more invariably slows reaction time and impairs good judgment. For the same reason, sexual desire is increased, but at the same time sexual performance is impaired.

Sport divers need every atom of good judgment they can mobilize. Sharp eyes and perfect orientation in a sudden moment of crisis might make the difference between life and death. Divemasters know this and usually run their schools under a *no-drinking* banner. One famous teacher who specializes in large classes says, "I line 'em up and smell their breath. If I catch a whiff of booze, I throw them out."

Finally, if you like to play around at the hundred-foot depth, never dive with a hangover. Experience teaches that it increases susceptibility to the bends and other nitrogen problems. Nobody knows why. To be safe, save your thirst for postdive festivities— and then drink moderately.

ANOXIA (HYPOXIA)

Anoxia is the result of too little oxygen in body tissues. For some reason, divers prefer the word *hypoxia*. It means the same thing.

Oxygen is almost the only element in the human body for which nature has not created a back-up substance. When the body's supply is cut off or even reduced below normal levels, there is trouble.

The first cells to suffer oxygen starvation are those of the brain. Within minutes, they begin to sputter like wet fuses, then they stop functioning, and presently they die. It happens in four or five minutes. If a victim's oxygen supply cannot be restored within that time, the brain is usually damaged beyond repair.

Two conditions contribute to anoxia. First, the air in a diving tank may not be what was ordered. By accident, a compressed air tank may have been filled with something other than pure air. Second, the diver commits the unpardonable sin of running out of air.

The consequence is a classic set of symptoms—the diver feels and behaves as though he is drunk. His mind meanders tipsily at first, then wildly. His reflexes slow and his coordination decays. If he tries to walk on the bottom, he staggers like a drunk in slow motion. His lips may turn blue, but he feels gay and euphoric as though he is riding a water-borne marijuana high. It can happen in the blink of an eye. If the diver is experienced or lucky, he may recognize what is happening, because salvation lies in regaining control of the mind, which takes a huge dose of willpower. Rising a little toward the surface may help. Once the surface is reached, the best treatment is plenty of fresh air. If the victim is unconscious, give artificial respiration. If a portable bottle of pure oxygen is handy, administer some of it. Every inhalation will draw in oxygen and raise the level in the circulating blood. Aqua-docs say recovery can take place in a few minutes, but the victim shouldn't do any more diving that day.

ASTHMA

Olympic swimmer Rick Demont, an asthmatic, won a gold medal in the 1972 Olympics. He had swallowed a common drug before the race to prevent an attack. A straightlaced committee called his drug illegal and took away his gold.

Half the Australian swimming team of 1968 had asthma. Not long ago, the entire interior line for the Houston Oilers was asthmatic. What does it all mean? It means that asthmatics can be top athletes and winners. But can they be scuba divers? Not yet, apparently.

Let's look into a typical set of asthmatic lungs. The airway descends from the mouth through the trachea, splits into twin bronchial tubes that run to the right and left lungs and then divides further into smaller and smaller passages called bronchi.

These bronchi are an asthmatic's battleground. Muscle-covered, those tiny tunnels are peppered with cells that somehow react violently to such stimuli as dust, smoke, or even a change from hot to cold. Oddly, they can also be triggered by excitement, exercise, fear, or stress. When they react, they exude a thin white liquid. Swelling and weeping, they partially block the passage of air. During serious attacks, asthmatics turn bluish about the lips and fingernails. They cough almost continuously. Surely, no physician or divemaster is about to permit any such pitiable case to don a scuba outfit.

Up to now, nobody has offered air guaranteed to be pure. Up to now, no drug has been developed that insures against an asthma seizure during a diver's bottom time. Up to now, neither the medics nor the big diving associations dare to recommend scuba activities for asthmatics.

Some day, however, it's bound to happen. Dr. Lawrence Lamb writes, "Swimming seems to be a particularly good exercise for asthmatics." Once, even swimming was verboten. Today, it is endorsed. Perhaps, diving is only just beyond the horizon. For now, however, PADI, the YMCA, and all the other scuba sponsors agree that it is best for seriously affected asthmatics to stay up top (maybe with a mask and snorkel) in that nice warm water.

ATHLETE'S FOOT (EPIDERMOPHYTOSIS, TINEA PEDIS)

You've got it again, just like nine out of ten of the men in America. The first time, it probably was a dry scaliness between the fourth and fifth toes, those that are closest together; but this time the skin is fissured with white patches like grains of rice covered with skin and weeping blisters. It burns and itches. Scratching makes it worse. Usually, it is most severe between toes, but occasionally it moves around to beneath the arch. Or a toenail may be attacked, changing color to yellow-brown or turning opaque where it had been clear.

Athlete's foot packs a one-two punch. First, you're hit by a fungus jab. Second, you're walloped by a bacterial haymaker. The basic cause is wet skin. Dry skin normally has a thin acidic mantel or covering that keeps bacteria at a distance. Wet skin dissipates the acid, negating its protection, and the microbes move in. If the attack is so furious that your glands swell and hurt, your case is serious.

To get rid of athlete's foot, both invaders must be repelled. An initial fungus attack can be discouraged by a good antifungal powder or salve. One of the best is Whitfield's ointment. Even better, doctors say, is a more expensive drug called Tinactin, which is an over-the-counter trade name for tolnaftate. The treatment of fungus-caused Athlete's foot involves (1) cleanliness; (2) dryness; and (3) a drug. Dryness is particularly important. After bathing, dry your feet totally. In the summer, wear sandals to assure plenty of ventilation. Get rid of those imitation leathers that trap sweat inside the shoe. Wear cotton socks, not synthetics.

If bacteria have succeeded in adding their woes to your toes, you must go one step further. The treatment of choice is a 20 to 30 percent solution of aluminum chloride. This is the same stuff you rub or roll under your arms to stop perspiration. It is available as a solution at your drug store. Use a swab or cotton ball to apply it between the toes twice a day, soaking the swab generously. Some pharmacists would rather sell stuff that comes prepackaged. In that case, ask your doctor to prescribe Drysol. It's aluminum chloride already mixed. When the whiteness and itchiness have disappeared, cut down to one application a day for a week, then discontinue.

Warning! Better not use aluminum chloride when the feet are damp or right after a shower. It stings. Also, don't apply it to an open sore. Instead, ask your druggist for a bottle of Castellani Paint. It's an over-the-counter (OTC) item that can be applied with a Q-tip.

As a result of this treatment, bacteria succumb gradually and you are halfway home. Then you must mop up the fungi. Tinactin is the OTC powder or salve that does it. Some victims try Desenex before anything else because it's cheaper. Their second choice may be Selsun Blue (a shampoo), also very cheap, which sometimes clears up the infection. Next in line, because of its higher price, is Tinactin. Whatever you use, after the last trace of disease vanishes, continue treatment, particularly if the weather is hot and humid. The recurrence rate is very high.

Alternatives? Some podiatrists advocate a boric acid soak. They dissolve one teaspoon of boric acid powder in a quart of warm water and soak the afflicated foot. If the infection is minor, several soaks should eliminate the bacteria, leaving only the lesser problem of scaly fungi.

Another solution that attacks both fungi and bacteria is potassium permanganate. This drug has been used by armies and explorers from the tropics to the poles. Dissolve a 300 mg tablet in three quarts of cool water and you will have the most beautiful purple solution you've ever seen. More important, it is germicidal, astringent, anti fungal, and also good for poison ivy. Make a sopping wet dressing and apply it to your toes. Your feet will turn purple, but the infection will vanish. The purple dye fades under applications of hydrogen peroxide.

Prevention

Athlete's foot is highly contagious, especially in shower stalls. If some member of your family has it, swab out your shower stall daily with Lysol or Pinesol. Examine your toes daily. And dust with powder.

We've already noted that athlete's foot thrives on dampness. Its fungi are everywhere—in the air, in clothing, on the ground, in the water. Dirty socks and tennis shoes are fertile breeding grounds, and tight or artificial-leather shoes induce foot sweating and encourage faster breeding.

Because divers spend much of their time walking on beaches and boat decks or sea and lake bottoms, potential infection is everywhere. When possible, wear scuffs or paper slippers. Some diving schools use foot-tubs (like those used in golf clubs) to control the hungry tinea pedis. Tubs are useless unless they are emptied and their solution renewed every hour. Otherwise, every user adds his own collection of germs, shards of fungi, and colonies of bacteria. Even the socks you put on after a diving expedition can carry bacteria into your home. Wear socks once only, and boil them before you use them again.

After a shower, save one end of your towel exclusively for your feet. Dry thoroughly. From your own can of fungicidal powder, sprinkle dust between your toes. Inspect your toes weekly. If you must wear your socks or shorts a second time or when they are still damp, dust them and yourself thoroughly with fungicidal powder.

If a four-week period of home treatments fails to clear up your itching and scaling, seek professional advice (some physicians cut that time to ten days). A doctor usually recommends a formula containing the generic drug gruseofulvin. Be patient, any treatment takes time. Be very patient if your toenails become involved. Cure of an infected toenail often takes months and even may require removal of the nail.

BACKPACKER'S PALSY

A backpacking cave diver has sounded a warning worth repeating. He states, "Some of us walk miles to find a dive site we like. We load stuff onto our backs and pack into the wilds like Chinese coolies. This is a warning. Don't do it. Several months ago, one of my buddies made one trip too many. He's still trying to regain the use of his legs."

The weight of scuba and camping gear can bruise certain unprotected nerve ganglia. Pack straps carry a lot of weight. When they cut into a backpacker's shoulders, they can cut off circulation and paralyze part of the nervous system. Strap pressure for a few miles is rarely serious; but when it lasts for hours, it can be very serious indeed.

Maybe you feel a pain in the shoulder, or an arm goes numb, then a leg. You notice that your hands are mottled or swollen. When that happens, shuck off whatever you were carrying and "take five" for a stint of stretching. Concentrate on shoulder shrugs, twists, and rotations. Ask your buddy to give you a neck massage. Find a level spot at the base of a sapling and stretch out on your back. Wrap your hands around the tree trunk and talk him into pulling your legs (literally) until he shakes and jiggles the kinks out of your spine.

Even though the pain continues, you may decide to go on. Reduce your load, even if you have to stash half of it beside the trail and pick it up later. When you get home, buy a new backpack, one that uses the hips instead of the shoulders for weight bearing. If pain continues through the next day, abandon your expedition in favor of a short cut to the nearest neurologist.

BLEEDING

We are concerned here about two kinds of bleeding. The first develops during a dive; the second results from an accident that happens on the surface.

Any bleeding discovered on surfacing calls for action to stanch it. Loss of blood threatens life. You've got almost six quarts (females have five) in your body. You need it all. If a dive victim is bleeding from the nose or mouth, almost certainly the source is either the middle ear, the nasal sinuses, or the lungs which have been squeezed so that tissue has ruptured.

Treatment

If a diver is unconscious and bleeding when he surfaces, use artificial respiration immediately. Get someone to wrap ice cubes in towels and apply them to his head and neck. Call a doctor and arrange transportation to his office. He'll probably know it already, but suggest politely that 55 cc of 50 percent glucose will probably prevent vomiting so that oxygen can be given.

Prevention

Self-discipline is the most important measure. Don't descend faster than your instructor recommends or faster than your experience tells you is safe. Don't hold your breath during an ascent. Follow your bubbles.

If you cannot clear your sinus passages or your Eustacian tube easily, cancel the dive.

If a cold hangs on or if you have a tenacious ear malady, stay topside. Don't tempt fate by hoping things will clear up. A ruptured eardrum under water is an unsettling affair. If you're unsure, go to the most experienced diver in your group and tell him how you feel. Follow his advice.

Identify the type of bleeding by its flow and color. A torn artery spurts and the blood is bright red. A ruptured vein flows steadily and the blood is purplish. Paramedics say that practically all arterial bleeding can be stopped if an attendant applies steady pressure. Don't panic.

Bleeding from a body wound requires an immediate response. Stopping it calls for these standard first aid measures:

Apply direct pressure to the wound. Use a folded sterile cloth, if possible. Otherwise, use a handkerchief, sheet, pillowcase, sanitary napkin, or whatever will serve to hold the wound's lips together and soak up blood. If the bandage becomes saturated, replace it with another. Continue the pressure for about ten minutes without interruption.

If the flow does not diminish, find a location on the heart-side of the wound where an artery can be pressed against a bone. Adequate pressure will throttle the flow. The body has twenty-two pressure points, but only a few of them are used today.

For lower arm and hand, the pressure point lies against the inside of the upper arm just below the biceps.

For the lower leg and foot, locate the femoral artery and press on the inside of the thigh and against the femur.

For head wounds, press against the carotid artery in the side of the neck just below the point of the jaw. Remember that pressing on both carotids at the same time will deprive the brain of oxygen. This can result in serious damage. Be sure one carotid is always free to feed the brain.

For a scalp wound, locate the artery that runs across the temple and press it against the skull.

For the upper thigh, jam your fist into the victim's groin, pressing hard where it joins the body.

Nature's way to curtail bleeding is clotting. Any physical hurt releases a chemical that causes blood platelets to form into clumps. As they turn into clots and finally grow into scabs, they seal the injury. Disturb a wound as little as possible. Think twice about removing a bandage that might loosen some clots.

When the flow ceases, lay a sterile pad over the wound or over the bandage used earlier and tape it down. Keep up the pressure by using an elastic bandage. Wrap it so you can feel the pulse (in arm or leg) in the part *away* from the heart. If there's no pulse, loosen the bandage.

If nothings else works, resort to a tourniquet. Use a heavy necktie, bandage, anything except a narrow band that will cut into the flesh. Some older first aid books suggest releasing a tourniquet for five minutes or so every half hour. Recent practice says this may be life threatening. Today's practice reserves the removal of the tourniquet to the doctor alone. Call a hospital, describe what you have done, and ask for instructions. Rapid transport to a dispensary is essential.

Remember that the lips of a wound requiring stitches should be closed within six or eight hours. Plan your hospital visit accordingly.

Finally, if you are slashed by a stingray, stitches probably should be postponed. The wound is sure to be dirty and likely to become infected. Doctors will usually treat it with an open pack. Its healing is slower but surer and safer.

BLISTERS

Blisters often seem to be harmless under their transparent domes of stretched, glistening skin. They are wolves in sheep's clothing. They can kill.

Anybody who moves can get them. Wherever the skin is rubbed, chafed, or twisted, they can appear. Ball players have them on their hands (so they wear protective gloves when they bat.) Joggers get them on their toes, or sometimes under a painful callous on the bottom of the foot. Divers get them on their heels from badly fitted flippers. Calvin Coolidge, Jr., sixteen-year-old son of the thirtieth president of the United States, got one playing tennis in tight shoes on the White House courts. It killed him. He knew he had a blister, but he did not know the blister had opened a passageway through which deadly germs would invade his body and create a fatal infection. Antibiotics and other effective bacteria-killers had not been discovered in 1924.

Any break in the skin can become a chink in your armor. You have three lines of defense. First, your skin wraps you in a continuous epidermal cocoon from head to foot. Second, your leucocytes (white blood corpuscles) devour any stray trespassers they encounter. Third, your lymphatic system, which is a network of sluiceways, washes intruders into filtering stations called lymph nodes.

Two breeds of blister concern us. First, the superficial, filled with plasma, the liquid component of your blood. Second, the deeper blood blister, which is filled with blood because the wound is deep enough to rupture tiny blood vessels between the layers of your skin.

Treatment

Your primary objective is to prevent the lesion in the skin from turning into an infected wound. The first step is to wash your hands and the blister site with soap and water or alcohol. The second step is to dispose of the liquid within the blister. With a sterile needle, puncture the blister along one edge enough to provide drainage for its liquid contents. With a sterile pad or cotton ball, press the dome of the blister down gently until the skin is against the raw surface beneath. Leave this skin intact—it is nature's bandaid. Apply an antiseptic solution or cream to the blister's surface and the skin nearby. Some authorities prefer only a wash of water and antiseptic soap. Finally, apply a sterile bandage and tape it down securely.

Incidentally, Dr. George Sheehan, the famous jogger and medical advisor, employs a briefer treatment. "If the blister is distended, I may drain it," he says, "but usually I do not take the skin off." He paints or sprays the area with tincture of benzoin, then applies a strip of Zonas tape. That's it.

In two or three days, examination will reveal a healing blister lying under a coverlet of dead skin. Cut this skin away with sterile scissors. Wash the area with antiseptic soap, cover it with a sterile bandage, and tape into place.

If the blister is filled with blood, follow the above directions, being extra careful to eliminate any chance of contact with germs.

If the blister ruptures, cracks, or tears so that its liquid drains off and the site becomes an invitation for microbes, it is best to cut away the loose skin. Treat the raw sore beneath it with meticulous, antiseptic care. Wash it well with water and hospital soap, bandage it, and apply germ-free tape. Again, the primary objective is to prevent an infection.

As long as a blister seems to be healing, merely keep it clean and protected from pressure. If it weeps, turns red, swells, or develops a sunburst of red streaks, infection has probably taken hold. If there is swelling and soreness in the lymph glands of your armpit or groin or behind your knee, go to the nearest medic promptly. He will probably take a culture to discover the exact breed of invading organisms and then prescribe antibiotics, hot soaks, bed rest, and no diving.

Prevention

If you ever feel an unusual hot spot on your heels, toes, or hands, investigate the area. If you anticipate a blister, cover the spot with some thin elastic tape such as Johnson & Johnson's Dermicil. It may offer adequate protection. Avoid thick pads and tapes. Nonswimming blisters usually are caused by shoes or socks that don't fit properly. If walking or jogging is part of your training program, rub Vaseline on each foot before hitting the trail or wear two pairs of socks—light cotton inside, thicker cotton or wool outside.

If a hot spot worries you, try a skin spray called Tuf Skin or a piece of moleskin. Whatever you tape to your foot for dry land exercise, always apply talcum powder afterwards. For use under water, try mineral oil or Vaseline. But easy does it!

Above all, take every blister seriously.

BRUISES

Bruises come in many hues, mostly yellow, purple, and blue. They usually take about three hours to develop fully, during which they swell and turn color. They often look alarming, but they are rarely dangerous. Any part of the body's flesh that lies over a solid bony structure is eligible for what doctors call a *hematoma,* a condition in which clotted blood beneath the skin is absorbed by the body at a very slow rate.

People react differently to a blow or bump—one person's hide turns sooty black while anothers produces only a pale olive memento. Favorite sites are the back, shoulders, hips, thighs, buttocks, and lower legs. Hands and toes usually are spared, unless a blow falls on a fingernail.

Common practice forbids taking aspirin for a week after suffering a severe bruise. Aspirin is an anticlotting drug, and its effect might work against the interior wound's healing.

The development of a hematoma can be a serious threat. If one becomes organized through the drainage of blood into a contused area, it might harden and become inflamed and painful. Feel for it with gentle fingers, seeking its edges. If it becomes so well-defined that you can detect a lump or feel its edges, it is time to visit a doctor. On occasion, certain hematomas persist without giving pain or trouble for weeks or months. Others must be reduced by the aspiration of blood through a needle or by surgical incision.

Treatment

Treatment is straightforwarded and directed toward stanching the oozings of ruptured blood and lymph vessels beneath the skin (see "Swelling").

Apply cold packs as soon as possible, or a cold water bag or cracked ice in a towel. Heavily salted water has been tried and found wanting. Salt lowers the temperature, but it can cause frostbite and additional deterioration of the tissues. Next, apply a compression bandage.

Back Bruises

Back muscles are poorly protected. Any activity from athletic training to tumbling off a curb can roll the unwary person onto his backside. When an average 150-pound body falls, the back absorbs a thrust of 500 pounds as it strikes the ground. The pain and swelling can be traumatic.

Treatment involves preliminary twists to see if the spine is involved. (Usually it is not.) If it is, get professional medical help. Otherwise, use ice massage, repeating it hourly for two or three days. When you decide it's time for heat applications, sit in a hot tub or hot whirlpool or use a hot water bottle.

After a hot treatment, run through daily hip bends, half knee-bends, shoulder shrugs, and twists to test and amplify your range of motion. Rest as much as you can.

Hip Bruise

A bruise on the point of the hip is usually so painful that it is disabling. Falls or collisions are generally responsible.

Rest is the first consideration.

Give serious thought to getting an X-ray. You might have a fracture.

If you suffer from a charley horse spasm of the hip muscles, treat it with the regular bruise therapy of cold followed by heat plus rest. Hold off on heat until pain has dissipated and swelling has diminished.

Once you've begun heat treatments, try a daily hip flexibility drill. Avoid running or running-type games (tennis, squash, racquetball) until the injury is completely healed.

Thigh Bruise

Two of the body's biggest muscles, one fore and one aft of the thigh's femur, make a likely site for direct-blow bruises. Often one is unable to extend the knee without severe pain. Don't try to. Give the injury total rest instead. If you must move about, rent a pair of crutches. Keep the injured leg from touching the floor. It will accelerate your recovery.

Bruised Buttocks

The backside can be the site of the body's biggest bruise and provide the greatest challenge in its treatment. Self-treatment is difficult because arms and hands are designed to work before the body, not behind it and because the area is difficult to see. If you opt for self-therapy, follow the pattern of cold treatment for forty-eight hours, hot dressings thereafter, and complete rest throughout.

Lower Leg Bruise

A bruise of the lower leg often occurs in contact sports, punishing fleshy calf muscle and causing a bloody flood to spread under the skin. Seriousness of the injury can be judged somewhat by observing these signs: Find the pulse in the ankle, if possible. If it is strong and firm, the outlook for a prompt recovery is good. If there's no pulse, if the area is black or yellow, swelling, and feverish, visit a physician.

Fingernail Bruise

A bruise under a fingernail is actually a blood blister. Apply ice water first to inhibit swelling, then hot water to relieve pain. Blood usually collects under the fingernail, which turns black and aches. Later the nail stops growing and loosens at the edges. Don't try to help it loose. Stick it back in place with a Bandaid or a bit of adhesive tape. Eventually, a new nail growing beneath it will push it out of the way.

BURNS

Many divers get sunburned. Not so many get fireburned. Yet, when it happens, it is useful to know what to do.

Burns are rated by physicians in order of depth:

First degree. The skin is reddened and painful but not blistered.

Second degree. The skin looks much the same, but blisters appear quickly.

Third degree. The skin has been penetrated and charred. Underlying tissue has been destroyed. If the burn has gone deep enough to consume the sensory nerve-ends, this most serious of all burns may cause no pain.

Treatment

Treatment of burns has changed. Gone are grandma's unguents, as well as drugstore therapy. Today, the preferred pain-killer is ice water. This change and others are the basis of some *don'ts* and *do's.*

1. Don't smear the burned area with yesterday's favorites such as lard, butter, baking soda, honey, milk, oil, sugar, lubricants, or greasy sprays, salves, or ointments.
2. Don't open blisters.
3. Don't tidy up a burned area by picking off charred skin or other debris.

Now, the "do's."

1. Have the patient lie down, feet elevated.
2. Trim clothing from around the burned area with scissors.
3. If clothing sticks, let it alone and cover it with a dry sterile bandage.
4. Anticipate swelling of body parts and remove rings, necklaces, and bracelets that might cause constriction.
5. Urge the victim to drink all the fluid he can handle. (The U.S.

Public Health Service warns that a badly burned person may experience shock and that the best antidote is cool water laced with one level teaspoon of table salt and one-half teaspoon of baking soda to the quart. He'll need, say experts, about ten quarts in the first twenty-four hours).
6. Keep the burn victim warm but not too warm. To cover a burned body, use a clean sheet with a light blanket on top.
7. Dressings recommended by various authorities are *(1)* a freshly laundered sheet, *(2)* a plastic sheet (like a painter's drop cloth, or a cleaner's garment bag), or *(3)* a blanket of styrofoam. The purpose of any sterile dressing is to prevent infection. Sometimes it is better to leave the burned area exposed to the open air.*

Treatment

For first degree burns, old-timers often want to use that standby of the past, white petrolatum (Vaseline). Certainly, it served them well. Today's consensus is that cold water not only washes away germs but also alleviates pain. Its temperature should be about sixty to seventy degrees, no warmer. (At sea, there's always a plentiful supply of water. Don't use it. The body absorbs the salt with potentially deadly results.) Lacking water, fill a paper cup with ice cubes and move it carefully over the burned skin. It may hurt a bit but the ultimate result is faster healing.

For second degree burns, skin blisters are their trademark. Heat has so disorganized the body's epidermis that internal fluids can force themselves to the surface to form bubbles. As long as a blister's surface is intact, however, no infection can enter your body through it. So protect it. If a blister has ruptured (or even if it hasn't), wash the area with antiseptic soap, rinse it, and continue until pain subsides. Then cover with a clean dressing. One school of thought suggests covering a burn with a plastic bag taped to the skin at the burn's edges to keep out air.

A do-it-yourself unguent that comes highly recommended for first degree and small second degree burns is the juicy gel of the aloe plant. A tropical member of the *Aloe vera* family, its succulent spikes grow in thousands of southern pots and herbal patches. Its soothing and healing powers are legendary. Cut a three-inch length of spike and squeeze its gel directly onto the

---

*These suggestions are adapted from *Emergency Medical Guide,* by John Henderson, M.D., New York: McGraw-Hill Book Company, 1978.

burn. Repeat as needed. Results—according to trusted users—are almost beyond belief.

For third degree burns, treatment demands careful protection against infection, protection from shock, and rushing the victim to a hospital or burn center.

Treatment must begin with securing transportation to a hospital. Don't worry about cleaning the burned area. Cover it with a sterile dressing, several thicknesses. Your struggle now is to keep infection from developing. If the area to be protected is large, consider a dressing of cellophane wrap or aluminum foil. Keep the victim warm. He's a potential shock case so he needs copious quantities of water. Administer all he can handle, one quart of cool water to one level teaspoon of salt and one-half teaspoon of soda.

Finally, *any* burn that involves the victim's hands, feet, face, or genitals requires a physician's attention, as does any patient with a fever of 101 degrees or more. It's a sign of infection.

CALLUSES

When you've got a foot callus, you know it. Its skin is thick, and usually it is yellow. You can feel it under your fingers: it is a *skin* callus if it's shallow, a *tissue* callus if it's deep and sore and you can feel a tiny, tender pealike formation in its middle. Regardless, you want to get rid of it as soon as you can, first for comfort, but more important because if you jog to keep in shape for swimming it can throw off your foot strike so that you can twist a bone out of shape or stretch a ligament.

Treatment

1. Soften the callus with baths.
2. Reduce the callus by abrasive rubbing.
3. Prevent future calluses by using the right shoes, pads, or other foot aids.

Foot Baths. Salt water is almost universally recommended. Use table salt or Epsom salts. Two cupsful in a *gallon of hot water*. Soak your calluses for at least twenty minutes. Some authorities recommend alternate hot and cold footbaths. After the footbath, rub the feet with baby oil, Vaseline, or Nivea cream oil. Massage the foot until the callus seems soft.

Reducing. Rub the callus pad down by using sandpaper, pumice stone, or a callus file that you can buy at a drugstore. Never pare a

callus with a razor blade. Be patient. Rub until your foot tells you
to stop. It may burn slightly or feel tender. Stop at the first sign of
going too far.

Padding. Paint the reduced callus with a good antiseptic to
prevent invasion of the site by fungi or bacteria. Protect the callus
with suitable pads. These can be cut from adhesive-backed foam
rubber, moleskin, or lamb's wool. Don't use absorbent cotton next
to the skin—it collects bacteria. Arrange your padding *around* the
callus site, never on top of the callus. The idea is to reduce pressure
and let the padding absorb the shock of your weight. Continue the
bathing-rubbing-reducing treatment two or three times per week
until the site is normal.

Prevention

A callus forms on your foot when something is wrong. The
abnormality can be flat feet, fallen metatarsals, hammer toe, a
subcutaneous calcium deposit—for a jogger—running on the
wrong side of the road.

A callus is formed either by friction or by shearing force.
Friction happens when shoes are too large and cause a slippage or
when bones press on an unyielding surface and displace the skin
with every foot strike. In self-defense, the skin reacts, thickening
and toughening. The reaction is useful if you are a Hottentot and
wear no shoes. If you wear shoes, the eventual result is pain.

Shearing action takes place when the skin does not shift, thus
transmitting the torsion and tension of body motion to layers
deeper within the flesh. This happens to the hands of persons who
grip baseball bats, tennis racquets, golf clubs, axe handles, and
carpenter's hammers.

It also happens to persons who walk. The usual foot callus
develops on the ball of the foot behind the big toe. Body weight
causes it, coming down heavily on the metatarsal bone (there are
five of these, one for each toe) and squeezing it between the sole of
your foot and the sole of your shoe. Since the big toe receives the
impact of most of your weight (multiplied by three if you are
running), it follows that the big toe's metatarsal is the worst
troublemaker. At first, the fat beneath your skin on the bottom of
your foot tries to absorb the stress but repeated blows flatten it to a
hardened layer with no elasticity. In time, the callus may crack or
split or become infected. Common sense says you must prevent it.

Fortunately, prevention is possible. Place a metatarsal pad
(available at any Dr. Scholl's display) under the foot's *second*
metatarsal head and tape it in place. This maneuver makes the

second toe more prominent and divides the impact of your weight between it and the big toe. The callus now has a chance to improve. If it doesn't see a physician or a licensed podiatrist.

About one-third of all humans are said to have Morton's foot, a foot in which the second toe is longer than the big toe. Doctor Morton discovered that it caused problems. Mother Nature's intent was that the big toe, because of its size and placement, should do more of the foot's work than any of its four companions. A long big toe seems to help swimmers and sprinters. If you have Morton's foot, the big toe throws more work on the adjacent second toe, driving its metatarsal against the shoe sole and creating a callus behind it.

The remedy is simple. Increase the weight-bearing prominence of the short big toe by placing a pad under its metatarsal and taping it in place. Thus, the first and second toes become the partners they are supposed to be, and a callus is prevented.

CHAFING

Chafed skin is pink or reddish and usually wet. Chafing occurs when two body parts rub together. Or its cause can be a wet suit that is too tight or flippers that are too loose. In short, it is inflammation caused by friction. Perspiration compounds it. Grains of sand multiply it. The end result can be itching, burning, and swelling. Medics call it *intertrigo,* which means to rub.

Treatment

Looking at the weeping inflamed skin, you'll be tempted to smear on a cream or lotion. Forget it! The best treatment is a simple wash with soap and water three times daily. Use a drying powder to control weeping or any excess of moisture. Ask the druggist for a good antiperspirant. Among those most often recommended are: Dry Ban, Arrid Extra Dry, Manpower Superdry, Right Guard antiperspirant, Dorothy Gray Roll-on, and Antiperspirant Roll-On. If recovery is slow or you see signs of infection, wash with rubbing alcohol and let dry, then powder.

Prevention

Prior to a training workout, be certain that you are dry under the arms, between the legs, and wherever friction might develop between flesh and flesh or between flesh and fabric. Prior to a dive, apply Vaseline to bothersome areas.

Some divers cover the inseams of their wetsuits with a smooth, soft tape to prevent friction at the crotch and elsewhere. Others place a sheet of cotton under the jockstrap so that its edges are padded.

After a dive, (1) wash the site with soap and water; (2) dry thoroughly; (3) if improvement is slow or worsening, paint with alcohol; (4) dust with antiperspirant powder.

CHARLEY HORSE

You've had a hard blow in the area of the thigh. You can feel a tender, painful, swollen area. You limp. You cannot run. Actually, it's a super muscle bruise. The muscle on top of the thigh is called the quadriceps, and it runs from the knee to the hip. Made up of four separate muscles, its tension keeps you standing.

Originally, only a contusion of the muscle atop the thigh was known as a charley horse. Nobody knows where the name came from or who Charley was! This muscle bruise takes place when the blow falls upon a fatigued or relaxed muscle. In appearance, it may range from badly to slightly swollen. Its color (blue, yellow, purple) may be that of a typical bruise, or it may show nothing at all.

Try a strength test with the bruised muscle. A charley horse reduces it amazingly. See if your strength is normal or less than normal. Also, what has happened to your range of motion? Any decrease is a cause for concern.

Classifications of injury are first degree—tenderness at site of impact, little restriction of range of motion; second degree— swelling at point of impact, restriction of knee flexion; third degree—tenderness and swelling, marked restriction of knee movement, bad limp.

Some authorities say the charley horse occurs in muscles other than the quadriceps. Some say it happens as a result of a violent muscle tear. Regardless, everyone agrees on the treatment: rest, compression, cold compresses, leg elevation.

Treatment

Ice packs should be applied for at least thirty minutes, followed with elastic bandaging spiraling from groin to knee. Some train- ers use large rubber pads under the spiral bindings. Other experts use ice packs continuously for forty-eight hours then switch to elastic compression dressings and leg elevation for forty-eight hours. Use crutches to stay off the injured leg. If possible, seven to ten days bed rest at home is a boon.

Start physical therapy only when pain, swelling, and tenderness are gone, usually at the end of seventy-two hours. Therapy can be hot packs or thirty minutes in a whirlpool, followed by massage. The technique of ultrasound seems to be replacing massage. Try exercising the leg to pain tolerance once every hour for five minutes, moving the joints as soon as it doesn't hurt. No walking or bearing full weight until you can extend your knee against ten to fifteen pounds of resistance.

If the thigh does not respond in three to four weeks, suspect myositis (a deposit of calcium in the injured muscle). X-rays will tell if this is so. A doctor will tell you what to do.

CHIGGERS

Up North, these nearly invisible pinkish mites are called chiggers. Down South, they are red bugs. After they bite you, they spit a kind of juice under your skin that dissolves flesh into a bloody brew they suck back into their bodies.

They feed on almost anything that moves, including birds and snakes; but they love humans, especially picnickers who sit in the grass, backpackers who follow weedy trails, and lovers who frequent cemeteries. Once they have migrated from a weed patch to a warm body, they seek a cozy spot in which to feed. Favorite places are beneath tight clothing such as belts, bras, garters, tight wristlets and socks. Apparently, a chigger dinner continues for three or four days, after which—when their skins are plumped out with human tissue—they withdraw their fangs and return to the jungle.

You become aware of them about twenty-four hours after their first meal. Usually a persistent itch announces their settling in and a spreading red blotch designates their dining area. A folk myth holds that they bury themselves beneath the skin where they feed and die. Not so. A powerful magnifying glass will disclose a chigger, only its head buried in a hair follicle or pore, its exposed pink body filling with the victim's blood.

Chiggers are not a menace; they are a nuisance. They do not transmit a disease; but they raise blisters that can become infected. And they itch and itch and itch!

Treatment

Dab each bite with a cotton ball soaked in antiseptic. Get a small bottle of isopropyl alcohol from your druggist and paint the area with it. It kills red bugs and stops the itch for a while, but don't expect too much. The itching agent is under your skin in the juice injected by the chigger. There's no way to get it out.

If you've got rubbing alcohol in your medicine cabinet, rub it on. Some creams will help. Our choice includes Nupercaine, Xylocaine, and a cortacosteroid concoction called Aristacort. If you ever suspect that you are in chigger country, visit a local pharmacy and ask the man what works for his customers. If you're in the wilderness or on a tropic isle, scratch if you must—but never with dirty fingernails.

Prevention

Local residents will warn you about any turf you may be visiting. Ask if the territory is infested. Better still, test it for yourself. If you contemplate settling down in an unfamiliar area, take a six-inch square of black cardboard and prop it on its edge in a patch of grass. Nature guides swear that a mysterious force draws chiggers to such a card and up its face to a kind of town meeting on its topmost edge. They say you can see them by the score. If you still intend to picnic, spread a drop cloth first.

Prevention should begin before you step out of the house. Some backpackers sprinkle sulphur in their shoes with good results. Others rely on insect repellants such as Off, Six-Twelve, and Cutters Spray. Apply it on your shoelaces, around shoe tops, socks, and on all bare skin below the hips.

After exposure, take a hot bath, make a heavy lather, and rub it all over the body. Repeat three or four times. Towel briskly. Not many chiggers can survive such an assault.

JET LAG

Round-the-world divers, take note. Doctors call it *circadian dysrhythmia,* and it is neither an injury nor a disease but it can deliver a knockout punch. The word *circadian* comes from a Latin phrase, *circa dies,* which means "about a day"; and circadian rhythms are the body's normal functions (hunger, sleepiness, and the like) that occur in twenty-four-hour patterns. Circadian dysrhythmia is a mystery malaise. Symptoms include loss of appetite, dizziness, fatigue, overpowering drowsiness, blurred vision, and nausea. Divers, athletes, and other travelers call it jet lag. Its cause is travel east-to-west or west-to-east across five or more time zones. North-to-south travel, as from New York to Caribbean diving resorts, seems to carry no such penalty.

The earth has its ocean tides. The human body also has its tides, most of which are tuned to the world's daily bath of sunshine. A basic body tide is your twenty-four-hour cycle of sleep and rest. Another tide causes your body temperature to rise and fall at the same hours each day. Secretions from your adrenal glands, it has been discovered, ebb and flow in rhythm with the solar system.

Alarm clocks start the work day in England six hours earlier than they start it in New York. When a traveler violently alters his waking and sleeping schedule, he sets up an imbalance that apparently confuses many of his vital functions: clarity of mind, for instance; peak physical performance, for another. Our State Department now urges shuttle diplomats to postpone negotiations until they have passed at least twenty-four hours on the other fellow's turf. Olympic athletes flying to Japan or Europe have been advised to arrive three weeks ahead of their meets to allow their bodies to adjust. One full day for recuperation seems to be the least in which the body can readjust. G.F. Catlett, writing in *Modern Medicine* magazine, recommends this four part plan:

1. Depart well rested.
2. Choose a daylight departure.
3. Eat and drink moderately before takeoff, during the flight, and after arrival.
4. Plan no demanding physical or mental activity for the first twenty-four hours.

We know a transatlantic sports diver who invented his own anti-jet-lag remedy. He set his alarm clock ahead by one hour on each of the last six days prior to his eastward departure. When he joined his friends in London, he had already adjusted to their rhythm; he was ready to eat and sleep when they did; and he could don his scuba tanks with all his juices at full tide. Not once since, he asserts, has he been bothered by circadian gremlins.

This plan has worked for some, not for others. If your trip is too sudden for such deliberate preparation, wisdom suggests trying to spend your first twelve hours after arrival in bed.

COFFEE

How does coffee get onto a list of diving maladies? It's not an injury, an ailment, or an accident waiting to happen? Or is it?

If you are one of the Americans who help drink up 70 percent of the world's coffee production, consider these possibilities. Depending on how much coffee one drinks, scientific research indicates, it can cause such abnormalities as burning in the stomach, belching, ulcers, diarrhea, fast pulse, skipped beats in the heart, elevated blood pressure, ringing in the ears, insomnia, trembling, sweating, irritability, anxiety, higher blood pressure, indigestion, fatigue, tension, depression, and a tendency to burst into tears.

Dr. Larence E. Lamb calls coffee "a liquid go-pill." Caffeine, its main drug, stimulates the central nervous system. Those amphetamines called goof balls do the same thing.

The good news is that coffee stimulates the brain. Ideas flow, fingers fly, and typists increase their speed and reduce their mistakes under its influence. It is interesting, however, that this improvement applies only to old, well-rehearsed routines. Stimulated by coffee, a new skill deteriorates.

When does coffee become dangerous? When have you drunk too much? Each individual has his own level of tolerance. Most surveys say the danger level is at four to six cups. Some studies show no penalty even beyond that intake. A few experts assert that damage is done by the very first cup.

If you are a diver and love coffee, experiment until you find your own level. If coffee enables you to make faster, better decisions, okay. But remember that you are definitely using a powerful drug. The stuff stimulates your adrenal glands, which pour out an incredibly potent stimulant. If your body handles the drug just right, it can make you a winner. If you misjudge, it can push you into a heart attack.

Caffeine is also found in colas, tea, cocoa, and chocolate. Maybe every diver would be wise to monitor his own and his dive buddy's caffeine intake. Underwater, a hopped-up caffeine-head is a menace.

Caffeine levels in drinks were measured recently by a famous Boston research organization. You can rely on their figures.

Coffee, brewed: 80 to 120 milligrams of caffeine per cup.

Coffee, instant: 66 to 100 milligrams.

Tea, leaf: 30 to 75 milligrams.

Tea bags: 42 to 100 miligrams.

Tea, instant: 30 to 60 milligrams.

Cocoa: up to 50 milligrams per cup.

Cola drink: 30 milligrams per 8-oz. can.

Chocolate bar: 25 milligrams.

A final word: Coffee speeds one's metabolism by about 10 percent, accelerating heart rate and respiration. This uses up precious air and shortens bottom time. Worse, coffee acts on some persons by magnifying the urge to go to the bathroom.

Coffee in moderation does not kill. Taken at the right time, it gives a lift to worn spirits. For most experienced divers, the right time is after the dive, not before.

COLDS

Why discuss the common cold in a book devoted to fitness and the accidents of sport diving? Because it is America's most neglected illness, because everybody, but *everybody,* catches colds, and because divers hate them with special virulence.

A cold is an inflammation caused by a virus. It hits the membranes of the nose, throat, pharynx, and tonsils. The viruses travel widely, reaching into the inner ear through the Eustacian tube and into the chest. A diver with a congested Eustacian tube is as miserable as a clam out of water.

Kids average about six colds per year. Adults average two. Adult parents have more colds than adults without kids. Exposure makes the difference. Remember that word—exposure!

Never forget that the cold is a contagious disease. Sneezes and nose-blowing spread germs over many feet. Bob Kiphuth, famous swimming coach at Yale, tried to prevent germs spreading among his swimmers by forbidding nose-blowing. Instead, they inhaled the mucus into their nasal passages and discharged it through the mouth. Believe it or not, his teams rarely caught colds.

Dr. Lawrence E. Lamb says, "Actually the hand is the biggest offender. Why? Because the germs get on your hand and then you touch your face." What does he tell you to do? "Wear gloves when you go out, and when you return take your gloves off and wash your hands. That way you avoid germs on doorknobs and other places."

Treatment

Since the cause of colds is exposure, the best preventive measure is to avoid exposure. It isn't easy.

The next best medicine is rest—not staying in bed all day, necessarily, but taking a morning nap, an afternoon snooze, and getting to bed early at night.

Ordinarily, there's no need to see a doctor unless you want someone to hold your hand. He may prescribe a drug or two, but you can get the same thing over the counter. Treat yourself to fluids: orange juice (the real stuff, not a watered-down version), tea, soups. If you can buy some horehound leaves, brew them into a hot tea. It keeps the mucus thinned. Feverish? Drink all the liquid you can. If every move is an ache, take aspirin—10 grains every four to eight hours. If aspirin upsets your stomach, use Tylenol, the over-the-counter drug, acetaminophen, and take it as you would aspirin.

Vitamin C is controversial, despite Nobel Prize Winner Linus Pauling's book, *Vitamin C and the Common Cold.* Many athletes swear by it. So does Pauling. The American Medical Association and the average doctor do not.

If sore throat is a normal complication of a cold, a strep throat is a disaster. Take a mirror and a flashlight and look down your own throat (or your patient's) and if you see a bright red or scarlet-spotted membrane, you have a real problem. To deal with strep throat you need professional help—and powerful drugs. Call a doctor fast!

What about using an OTC decongestant to reduce the swelling that blocks the entrance to your Eustacian tube? Their packages hint at blockage-free diving. Beware of such promises. Although many dive shops stock these decongestants, some do not. Some divemasters say they simply don't work, or worse than that, they are a menace. A decongestant may decrease the swelling that blocks a Eustacian tube but such a drug eventually wears off. Moreover, there's a rebound reaction that sometimes causes recently shrunken cells to puff up bigger than ever. If that happens under water, a diver can be in for a painful blowout of his tympanic membrane.

Two recommendations: Skip all decongestants; skip the dive any time you cannot clear your Eustacian tubes.

Prevention

In order to prevent re-exposure to one's own cold, use tissue instead of a handkerchief.

Wipe off doorknobs.

Never drink from a public dipper or water glass.

Never overuse yourself physically. Many divers have noted that they catch cold after prolonged diving expeditions. Marathoners by the thousands contract colds after a race. Their body cells are really sending a signal: "Take it easy, buster. We're at the end of our rope." Stress causes colds. Oddly enough, cold doesn't cause colds. Arctic explorers don't catch colds until they return to civilization.

Everybody seems to have a remedy. Mountaineers in Appalachia drink tea made from pine needles. Or they parch red pepper, powder it, and brew it. Others mix honey and whiskey and drink it neat.

Some athletes think that superb physical conditioning can prevent colds. Wrong! "Magic" Johnson and Willie Stargell get colds like everybody else, but they usually recover faster.

COLD WATER AND CHILLING

There's a saying, "No matter where you dive, if you stay down long enough, you are going to get chilled." Let's look at that statement.

The body's temperature averages 98.6° F.

Water temperature around the world runs from 28° in the Arctic Ocean to 85° in the tropics. On the American East Coast, it may average 77° on the surface, drop to 59° or 60° at a depth of 1,500 feet, and plunge down to 39° or 40° at 4,000 feet. That's cold.

Fresh water in lakes and quarries collects in layers that are cold, colder, and coldest. Some quarry bottoms run a temperature of 36°. Each layer is different, the greatest temperature change coming in the top 15 feet, where the sun's rays penetrate. Many divers know the feeling of sinking through a zone as warm as soup and suddenly tensing under the impact of an ice bath. The boundary between the two layers is called a thermocline. Sometimes, there's a 20-degree drop. Be aware of it. It can cause a shock to which the body reacts violently.

In diving, cold water is the body's natural enemy. It draws heat from the body's tissues at a rate twenty-five times faster than air. Most divemasters insist on their students wearing an exposure suit that will delay the process. A foam neoprene suit is effective in water above 50°. Below that, a dry suit should be worn over warm underwear. Evidence exists that immersion in freezing water has killed people within a couple of minutes. Even prolonged exposure in comparatively warm water—like 65°—can kill. In order to sustain your life, your core temperature (at the center of your body where all your vital organs are housed) must register within a few degrees of 98.6° average. Even a few degrees of reduction of the core temperature results in *hypothermia*. At 95° you lose much of your mental functioning and don't know where you've been or what you are doing. Researchers who have undergone Navy tests at that body temperature found that they were unable even to open a jacknife. At 94°, the brain surrenders to amnesia.

Hypothermia is sneaky. It can bring on an irresistible fatigue. The slightest effort becomes a monumental task. Divers working around deep offshore reefs have returned to the breaker line too tired to struggle through the surf. Others have surfaced into a strong wind or current that swept then to their deaths.

Treatment

Treatment consists of the swiftest possible warming of a diver's body. Draw a tub of hot water. Check it with a thermometer to be sure it is under 110°. Soak the victim for about a half-hour. If he is conscious, serve him hot drinks—noncarbonated and nonstimulating. No coffee or whiskey! Some authorities suggest beef broth or sugared water.

If no tub is available, pour warm water into the victim's unzipped wet suit so that it gets between his skin and the neoprene. Or stand him under a hot shower. As a last resort, wrap him in hot towels or sheets.

Finally, insist on bed rest.

Prevention

Be aware that you may be one of those allergic persons for whom sudden immersion in icy water is as damaging as a gigantic bee sting.

Be aware that you are losing heat calories every minute you remain in water even under the most favorable conditions.

Be aware that under water your energy ebbs at a rate about twenty-five times faster than would be the case on land.

If you plan a deep dive, first eat a nutritious meal with plenty of carbohydrates for energy.

If you begin to shiver before your deep-water assignment is completed, swim up through the thermocline to a warmer level and rest a bit. Treasure divers do this many times during a work session.

If your shivering continues or becomes uncontrollable, begin your ascent and leave the water. Experience shows that most people shiver when their core temperature drops to about 96°. That's alien territory. Rap on your air tank to get your buddy's attention, grab yourself around the chest in the classic "I'm cold" signal, close your fist and point up with your thumb. Then cautiously follow your rising bubbles to a warmer climate.

CORAL

Many a novice diver blunders into a pile of coral thinking it is a heap of rocks. Instead, it is an ancient mound of skeletons, layer on layer, of what were once tiny, jellylike animals called polyps. Each generation has added its height and breadth to the vanished life below. North of Australia, the Great Barrier reef has grown to a length of 1,250 miles.

Despite their incredible colors, despite their fantastic resemblance to mushrooms, fans, cathedrals, and castles, corals are not a diver's best friend. Old coral is harsh and unbelievably abrasive. Living coral can sting. Only some coral is as soft and harmless as a puppy's nose.

The stinging corals are hydroid coral, millepore coral, and fire coral. The first trails a small creamy tendril through adjacent waters. If you blunder into it, it stings defensively. The second has been called the poison ivy of the sea. If you brush against it, your skin becomes ruddy, thickens, and develops a violent rash. Fire coral is really not coral at all but a member of a different species that looks and acts like coral. It actually is a tiny multicelled doughnut equipped with vicious stinging cells. Dropping one's bare hand onto a fire coral colony is akin to smacking it down on a red hot stove.

Finally, and fortunately, most coral is stone dead, long ago turned into the flinty pillars of calcium carbonate that underlie practically all the world's warm-water sea gardens. Rock hard, sharp edged, and usually slime covered, it can tear the skin like barracuda teeth. Given an opening, slime-bred microorganisms can penetrate your body. The infection that results is called coral poisoning.

Treatment

The objective is to prevent or minimize infection. Treat coral poisoning as you would an open wound. Wash it with soap and water. Cleanse it with hydrogen peroxide. Apply a sterile bandage. If the stings produce welts or lesions, use a cortisone or antihistamine ointment. Meat tenderizer (papain) mixed with water is standard treatment for the bites of land-based insects. For coral infection, ask a doctor to consider prescribing Panifil ointment. It is ready-to-use papain and seems to accelerate healing.

Prevention

If you are diving in coral country, wear boots, gloves, and long underwear or jeans. Avoid contact with all that fiery beauty. Beware of deep currents that can toss you into a coral reef. Don't follow fish or lobsters into coral-edged caverns or cul de sacs. Remember that the hides of sea creatures have been toughened by centuries of deep-sea hide-and-seek. After only forty years or so of scuba, man is still a thin-skinned land creature.

CRAMPS

Tight fins can cause cramps.

So can overtaxed calf muscles or hamstrings and gastros (gastronemius muscles), eating the wrong foods, and exercising too soon after a big meal.

Cramps hit swimmers of every age, in and out of the water, before and after diving.

Worst of all were swimmers cramps, according to the medical gossip of the last century. Stomach cramps! The victim was struck with a spasm, reduced instantly to helplessness, and sank like lead to the bottom. Did it really happen?

Not so, say modern researchers. Those were old wives' tales; but for many years they created such an atmosphere of fear among beginning swimmers that many did lose their lives without a struggle. Charles E. Silvia, Springfield College coach, who studied the subject exhaustively, reported: "In over 25 years of experience with swimming and swimming men, I have never seen one stomach cramp, or met a dependable swimming man who has seen one."

What is a cramp?

"A sudden, painful involuntary contraction of a muscle from a chill, strain, etc.,"—says one dictionary about that swift, hardening, paralyzing, tormenting muscle spasm that can strike thirty-five separate locations in the human body. Fingers and toes become cocked helplessly, agonizingly. A foot freezes into immobility. A debate has raged for years about the cause of cramps. Many reasons are proposed. So are remedies. Some of the today's common causes:

Cold water stimulates overbreathing that expels so much carbon dioxide that the blood turns alkaline. When alkaline blood feeds into a muscle, it triggers a nerve spasm which turns that muscle into a block of agony.

Loss of salt through excessive sweating.

Exhaustion or fatigue that prevents relaxation.

Overusing muscles while walking, jogging, or swimming. (After a long race, swimmers have reported finger cramps that cupped their hands exactly as they are used in swimming.)

Too much coffee.

Lack of balance among such body minerals as calcium, magnesium, sodium, and potassium.

High heels.

Decreased circulation in the legs.

Varicose veins (impaired circulation).

Diuretics (which reduce the body's liquid content).

Hot weather exercising.

Diarrhea.

Treatment

Of themselves, cramps do not need professional care. Doctors will usually try one drug after another, hoping to find something that works. You can do the same thing.

Here are treatments that have worked for some people.

Quinine sulphate is sometimes useful for controlling leg cramps. Dr. Acorse Thompson, Falls Church, Maryland, has used quinine successfully. Dosage: one tablet before bedtime. If cramps continue, try one tablet after dinner as well.

Many doctors have been successful with Vitamin E, but nobody knows why. Dosage is 400 to 800 international units before retiring.

Benedryl—an OTC drug—is an antihistamine that seems to suppress cramps. Nobody understands it, but many use it. Dosage: 50 to 100 mg in a pill or capsule at bedtime.

Warmth—lack of warm blood flowing through a muscle results in a "sensitized" muscle. Feet and legs are far from the heart. Hot and cold sensors in our nervous system are comparatively rare below the hips, so we wrap comforters about our shoulders but leave our limbs unguarded. Cooled leg muscles, already on the borderline, go into spasm, cramping painfully. Try wearing a pair of thin socks to bed. If they fail, try thicker ones, or a coverlet. Your objective is simply to keep your feet and legs warm enough to encourage normal blood flow.

Salt pills—if your cramps are caused by hot weather sweating (as in jogging or backpacking over forest trails). One researcher says that a backpacker on a hot, humid day may need as much as "three or four level teaspoons of salt to offset heat cramps." Salting one's food liberally is often effective. Or five-to-ten-grain salt tablets, coated to prevent irritation of the stomach. Or drinking salt water—one level teaspoon of salt to one quart of water.

Note that some authorities no longer believe that salt replacement with pills is useful. Stomach upset seems to be their principal objection. Your own cautious experimenting should provide the answer.

Replace your lost minerals. You lose them in sweat, urine, and feces. You can replace them by eating extra vegetables, grains, and fruits, and by drinking fruit juice.

Some crazier ways of eliminating cramps have also worked. They are supported by medical opinion.

For instance, if you get a cramp and want instant relief, try "acupinch." Pinch the skin of your upper lip hard (beneath the nose) between thumb and forefinger. Hang on until you feel the agony of the spasm diminish. Dr. Donald Cooper, a former Olympic team physician, has used this method effectively.

Finally, there's the paper bag approach. Save your small paper bags. When a leg or foot cramps, grab a bag in both hands, holding it securely to the mouth and breath into it. Exhale and inhale, rebreathing the air you have just exhaled. Continue until the cramp abates, which should be in ten or twenty seconds. The theory is that you rebreathe a large amount of carbon dioxide. CO_2 is a muscle relaxant. When your blood, supersaturated with carbon dioxide, reaches the cramping muscle, it relaxes them and the cramp vanishes. This remedy is included in a respected medical text used in many medical schools.

If nothing else works, visit a doctor for the sake of peace of mind. And if he finally reports, after various tests, that you've got an idiopathic cramp, don't panic. It's merely his way of saying he hasn't the foggiest notion of the cause of your pain.

Prevention

Cramp veterans have one excellent chance of beating their muscles. When Coach Silvia was studying the subject, he heard many victims report that "a cramp can usually be anticipated by the swimmer through the presence of a warning twinge." One physiologist stated, "If the affected muscle is fully stretched immediately after the warning twinge, the total cramp will be less painful and will disappear much sooner than if the traditional procedures of rubbing and kneading are followed."

Anticipate the stretch! Heed the twinge and contract the opposing muscles. If you're in water and a leg cramps, shift into a tuck float, grab a fin, and pull your foot upward (flexing) with one hand while kneading and massaging with the other.

CUTS

Every part of the body is likely to suffer a cut. Cuts are long or short, deep or shallow, clean or ragged. In games, most of them occur above the eyes or on the lips or tongue. In diving, they happen mostly to hands and feet.

A cut presents two immediate problems: first, to stop the bleeding;

second, to prevent infection. Any opening in the skin, no matter how small, becomes a point of attack for invading microorganisms.

Shallow cuts can be treated effectively at home or at the dive scene. Deep cuts, including puncture wounds and animal bites, require professional examination.

In general, cuts will not need suturing (stitches) unless they are over one inch in length. If suturing is necessary, it should be done within six or eight hours after the injury; otherwise, germs probably have penetrated your defenses and infected the wound. If a cut is small but the edges are jagged and cannot be brought together evenly and you don't want a scar, see a doctor.

If the cut is on an arm or leg, hand or foot, try to move each finger or toe. If you can't, a tendon may be severed (it can be repaired). If a finger or toe feels numb, a nerve may be cut. See a doctor (it will probably regenerate).

Cuts look worse than they are. Bleeding usually stops of its own accord unless arteries or veins are severed. An artery pumps bright red blood in small, regular spurts. A vein pumps dark red blood in a steady flow.

In shallow cuts, only tiny venules or slightly larger arterioles have been severed. They will seal themselves as soon as the blood clots (usually within an hour). Even if the penetration has severed an artery or vein, a pressure bandage or the elevation of the part (or both) will usually stanch the flow.

Pressure points are rarely used today as a means of stopping blood flow. Instead, professionals use a pressure bandage directly against the wound.

Whatever happened to the tourniquet? Once, all Boy Scouts and soldiers were taught to use it. Today's first aid warns against it because it represents a danger when it is left tightened too long. However, if bleeding is persistent and severe, use a broad necktie, bandage, or whatever is handy as a tourniquet while remembering that a limb without circulating blood is dying. *Loosen the tourniquet every ten minutes.* Once the bleeding is reduced, do not use it again.

Which is better for closing a wound, bandaging or stitching? A butterfly bandage can hold the lips of a small wound together as well as stitches. You'll probably need stitches if the bleeding cannot be controlled. You'll know from the blood that soaks through your bandages.

Maintain a lookout for infection that shows up from two to seven days after the injury takes place. Signs of infection are pain, marked swelling, drainage from the wound, red lines radiating beneath the skin, fever above 101 degrees.

Treatment

If bleeding is slight, start cleaning the wound immediately. Use soap and water. Sacrifice your instinct for gentleness for efficiency. Use a wet cotton ball, folded gauze, or a clean washrag.

If bleeding is moderate, apply an ice pack or cold compresses before cleaning the wound. An ice pack applied for ten minutes will be helpful.

If bleeding is severe, apply direct pressure over the wound using a clean handkerchief or a three-inch gauze bandage folded into a pad. Press it firmly against the wound for at least three to five minutes. Finally, apply a cold pack or ice.

Nowadays it's believed that antiseptics on raw tissue do as much harm as good. However, a good cleansing aid is hydrogen peroxide. Soak a pad in it and scrub, *stroking away from the wound* to avoid sweeping bacteria into it.

When the injury is clean, you are ready to bring its lips together. Butterfly bandages are ideal. They are available in suitable sizes from your druggist; or you can make your own of adhesive tape.

At this point, four hands are better than two; use two hands to pull the skin together while two other hands place the butterflies *across* the cut. When the cut is closed so that its lips meet in perfect union, make a pad of gauze that projects an inch or more beyond its edges. Secure the pad with adhesive tape.

Cuts inside the Mouth

Wash with cold water. Take a gulp and squish it vigorously around the tongue and teeth. Spit out.

You can do the same with a mouthful of hydrogen peroxide.

Follow with a preparation that is both astringent and antiseptic.

If swelling threatens or bleeding continues, hold a chunk of ice in the mouth against the cut.

Don't forget to examine the teeth to see if dental care may be required.

Cuts on Tongue and Lips

Cuts here require suturing if scars are to be prevented.

Cuts on the Face

Wash the skin thoroughly and carefully, remembering that it has been covered with perspiration and dirt. Use soap and water generously.

Because of the almost certain presence of germs (despite washing), use a mild antiseptic all around the wound, and then apply a medicated ointment that will keep the healing injury flexible.

Bring the lips of the cut together with butterfly bandages and affix a protective double fold of gauze bandage or a nonstick pad. Infection will remain a threat for several days. Watch for its signs.

Cuts on the Chin or Brow

These bony sites are often cut by a head bump. Treat them as above with this additional measure: Use cold compresses or ice over the site for ten minutes to prevent swelling.

Cuts on the Scalp

As always, wash with soap and water. Wash along the cut, not across. Use scissors to cut away nearby hair until you expose enough skin to attach a bandage.

Reduce the bleeding by using ice or an ice water compress, ethyl chloride, or an astringent. Apply an antiseptic along the lips of the cut and on adjacent skin. Finally, paint the site with a protective coating of elastc collodion and tape a sterile pad over the injury.

If the head wound is shallow, it will usually heal with home care alone. If it is more than a quarter-inch deep, see your doctor about it.

EARACHE

The average underwater earache is caused by unequal pressures operating against the eardrum. As is explained in the entry on ear squeeze, water pressure increases rapidly as a diver descends. An earache can occur even at the ten-foot level.

The eardrum is equipped with extraordinarily sensitive nerves. If water pressure against the outside of the drum exceeds the air pressure on the inside, the membrane is pressed inward and pain may result. Pain is a warning. Do not dive deeper when the ear hurts. Instead, ascend a few feet and try to pop your ears by closing your lips, grabbing your nose, and exhaling forcefully. Such maneuvers as swallowing and moving the jaw from side to side are often effective.

Most topside earaches are caused by infection, which may or may not be the result of an eardrum ruptured during a dive. Infection can begin in the outer, middle, or inner ear. Symptoms include pain ranging from annoying to excruciating, occasional dizziness, a "full" feeling in the ear, hearing loss, stuffy or drippy nose, headache, slight fever, ringing in the ear.

An external cause of inflammation can be a hard blow, the intrusion of foreign bodies into the ear canal, or careless probing with Q-tips or matchsticks. Its internal cause is usually a cold or some form of respiratory infection that travels from the sinuses or throat into the Eustacian tube where swollen tissue and phlegm create a plug that stops the flow of air between the nose and middle ear. This seals that chamber's only outlet so that the air pressure within can no longer rise or fall with the pressure outside the eardrum.

What has happened is this: The Eustacian tube, which runs from the throat to the inner side of the eardrum, is plugged by debris or swelling. The sealed cave of the middle ear (above the plug) becomes a breeding place for microorganisms. The body quickly mobilizes its white cells and carries them to the battleground where they try to destroy the invaders. Inflammation is a sign of this struggle.

In this situation, the use of drugs may be advisable, although each diver should be guided by his or her own tolerance to them any by his doctor's advice in taking them. The first line of defense consists of pain pills and decongestants. Good pain relievers, many physicians think, are the single-shot preparations containing either aspirin or acetaminophen. A decongestant may help to reduce the surplus phlegm that clogs the Eustacian tube. Decongestants are available as nose drops, sprays, pills, or capsules.

An infection of the middle or inner ear can be painful and dangerous. If it hangs on or worsens, get the best medical help you can find.

EAR, FOREIGN OBJECT IN

En route to your dive rendezvous, you got a bug in your ear. To you, he is a buzzing, tickling driving-you-crazy annoyance. Don't panic. Don't go after him with finger, pencil, or matchstick. Remember the ancient injunction: Never put anything in your ear smaller than your elbow.

Treatment

Insects like bright lights. Shine a flashlight's beam into the ear. Simultaneously, pull the earlobe downward and backward. It straightens the channel, encouraging escape. If no flashlight is handy, turn the ear toward the sun.

If your visitor is stuck in earwax, try to float it out. One method uses warm water and a syringe. If that fails, try heavier ammunition such as oil (baby, olive, or mineral), dripping it slowly into the canal, gradually filling it until the insect is removed. Keep working and tugging gently at your ear lobe. Never dig for an insect. The effort can drive it deeper; and a dead insect is harder to remove than a live one. Sometimes, just jarring the head with a cupped hand will do the trick.

Keep in mind that the obstruction may be a seed or a bark fragment. Water will make them swell, so postpone your dive until you've unloaded the unwelcome intruder, whatever it is. Remember! Gently does it. And don't be reluctant to visit your doctor.

EAR PLUGS

Never wear ear plugs while diving. They have no place in the sport of skin and scuba diving. Inserting an ear plug in the external ear canal creates a small air bubble, bounded at one end by the inner surface of the plug and at the other by the tympanum or eardrum. The air in this pocket is at surface pressure. As you dive, and as the water pressure increases, so does the tank air you are breathing, which flows from the mouth cavity up through the Eustacian tube to the inner ear. The result can be a ruptured eardrum.

SWIMMER'S EAR

Swimmer's ear is a catch-all designation for many kinds of ear afflictions. Since swimmers seem to have more ear problems than average, their sport gets the credit (or discredit). As a rule, water is to blame, but not necessarily because one swims. A shower can stimulate the same inflammation.

Swimmer's ear is the result of water being trapped in the ear. Sometimes a plug of wax will hold it there. Excessive dampness anywhere provides a breeding ground for fungus and bacteria.

If you suspect that something is wrong with an ear, have some one examine it for you. If wax accumulation does not hide the drum, a flashlight will reveal it. In good health, the drum will be shiny and as white as pearl. If it is diseased or irritated, it will show inflammation or redness over all or part of its surface. A bluish color may indicate fluid in the inner ear.

Not every ear drum can be easily examined. Some of us have curved canals that block off direct vision. If you are such a person, there's nothing to be done but to seek help from a specialist. He has the instruments for it.

Treatment

Treatment depends on how bad you hurt. The first move is to heal the ailing ear. The second to keep its inner recesses reasonably dry so microorganisms cannot find a foothold. Begin with a couple of aspirin tablets. That will take care of potential pain. Next, insert a tuft (a twist of cotton or gauze) saturated with Burrow's solution or diluted acetic acid. Don't drive it in hard; merely work it in until it feels nicely seated. Change this antiseptic plug every three hours. If you have a fever that rises higher than 101 degrees, or if pain increases, call your doctor.

From time to time, inspect the interior of the canal leading to the eardrum. Does it seem swollen? Is it red and juicy looking? If so, the inflammation can be treated by an over-the-counter antihistamine such as Sinutab, Allerest, Contac, or Sudafed. If the ear feels feverish, insert a drop of mineral oil. If distress lasts longer than ten days, call a doctor.

Prevention

Some persons are more likely to catch swimmer's ear than others. Their ear structures apparently admit and retain water more readily than the average. Since keeping the ear canal dry is essential to prevention, ear plugs may serve this purpose for surface swimming but never for diving. As stated before, ear plugs are very hazardous when used by scuba divers. Probably the best alternative is to dry the ear canals. Insert three or four drops of glycerine into each ear following your swim. Plug the canal with a slender cotton tuft and remove it after an hour. The glycerine absorbs the water and the cotton absorbs the glycerine.

COLD WATER EXHAUSTION

Water leeches heat from the body 25 times faster than air of the same temperature. Divemasters agree that smart divers must wear protective clothing when making drops into water colder than 72 degrees.

Underwater, don't be deceived by the ease with which you can move despite the cold. An exit through icy breakers or a stiff current can demand reserve strength that has already drained away without your knowing it. Individuals react differently to cold, but it is a safe rule to begin your ascent at the first sign of shivering. If you must dive again to complete an assignment, stay topside long enough to get thoroughly warmed.

If you are diving in the wilds, leave the water as soon as shivering begins, build a fire, and wrap up in all the necessary extra clothes and blankets available. And call it a day.

EXHAUSTION FROM OVEREXERTION

Symptoms of this condition include tiredness, nausea, dizziness, and almost always great difficulty in breathing. They often strike underwater, occasionally exploding into a moment of panic.

Actually, you are safe if you keep your cool. Your air supply is still intact. Your dive buddy is nearby to help. Let him know you are in trouble. Stop whatever you were doing. Turn your body into a statue that breathes deeply, slowly, deliberately. Presently, your breath will come easier and the alarm bells in your mind will stop clanging.

Prevention

Know thyself! Learn from experience what your body can do underwater. Ask that much of it and no more.

Treatment

Back on shore, oxygen to breathe and a supply of salty water to sip will usually produce a recovery. Watch for signs of shock. If recovery is delayed, seek a doctor.

EYE CUTS

Eye cuts are rare among divers because the eyes are protected by goggles or masks under water. On the surface, everyone is vulnerable. Flying objects abound, as do low tree limbs alongside rivers and lakes, not to mention fingernails and fingers that slip unexpectedly.

Treatment

Cuts over the eye are treated by lengthwise washing of the wound with antiseptic soap and water, application of an antiseptic, a butterfly patch, and a compression bandage. Go to a doctor for an examination and possible stitches. To stop bleeding and prevent swelling, apply cold packs.

If the eyeball itself is scratched or cut, cover it immediately with a sterile pad kept in place with a firm bandage wrapped around the head. Get to an ophthalmologist muy pronto. Eye scratches can turn into scars that limit vision.

EYE, FOREIGN BODY IN

A face mask protects a diver's eyes. So why this entry? Because you may have to reach the dive site over dusty roads, sandy beaches, or insect-infested trails. Suddenly, the wind blows and a foreign object closes an eye. Pain is followed by unbidden tears. A tear duct (one to each eye) spontaneously floods the afflicted tissue. You need fast do-it-yourself relief or your outing will be ruined.

Treatment

If the eye hurts badly, wash it with cold water. Resist the temptation to rub. Foreign particles can lodge under the lower lid (the most common site) or under the upper lid or become embedded in the surface of the eyeball. In any case, you are probably already crying, which is good. You will need all the tears you can muster. Lie down and grasp the lashes of the upper lid, dragging them down across the lower lid while you rotate your eyeballs in all directions. If the tears flow fast enough, the maneuver may wash away the foreign body.

If there's no improvement, wet a Q-tip and pull the lower lid down and toward your ear. This will expose the lower interior of the eye-socket. Using the penlight to illuminate the eye from the side look for a speck or a lash. With the Q-tip or the dampened corner of a handkerchief, remove whatever you find.

If there's still no relief, the irritant is probably under the upper lid. Now you must cooperate with your diving partner in a slippery but effective maneuver. While you look down, have your helper grasp the upper eye lashes and lift the lid away from the eyeball. Have him place a clean wooden matchstick or Q-tip stick across the lid's surface adjacent to the lashes. By pulling the elastic lid outward and upward will cause the lash boundary to curl back up and over on itself, exposing the lid's wet interior. Now your partner should be able to see whatever is lurking there and pick it up on a Q-tip. Don't worry about your laid-back eyelid. Look up at the ceiling and it will uncurl painlessly.

What if there's nothing to be seen under the upper lid? In a few cases, a foreign object will become embedded in the surface of an eyeball or the eyeball will be scratched. In either case, professional help is needed as soon as possible. Make a square bandage of gauze and tape it over the eye to keep out light and prevent blinking. Get to an ophthalmologist as soon as possible.

HEAT EXHAUSTION

Heat exhaustion has been the athlete's bugaboo for years. It happens when the body cannot get rid of its excess heat, which runs up the body temperature. One formula proposed by a celebrated physiologist says, "Never exercise vigorously when the temperature and the humidity are both over eighty."

The principle is simple. Exercise heats the blood, which is carried to the skin where sweat glands are activated. Evaporating sweat cools the skin, which cools the circulating blood, which cools the body. When the humidity is over eighty, evaporation slows so much that the cooling effect is negligible. And the blood goes round and round, getting hotter and hotter. The result is heat exhaustion.

Lugging air tanks across a beach is the kind of chore that creates heat. High water temperatures—above eighty—have the same effect. Topside, wear protective clothing, imbibe freely of cool drinks, and keep up your salt intake.

Symptoms of heat exhaustion include headaches, weakness, dizziness, and breathing difficulty. The skin turns clammy and cold and is covered with sweat. A sudden feeling of faintness is nature's warning to protect yourself.

Treatment

The condition is usually temporary. Pick a cool place, lie down, making sure that the head is lower than the body, and sip cold water for thirty minutes or so. If cramps hit or your muscles twitch, mix salt with your water or take a salt tablet. If recovery is delayed, seek a physician.

INTESTINAL GAS

You are ascending after a modest dive to sixty feet or so. All is well except for a sensation of fullness in the gut.

You slow your kicks, feeling a sudden pain down low beneath the ribs. As you try to flex the stomach muscles, the pain spreads into an agonizing belt about the abdominal wall.

You know the cause. It is gas in the gut. A compressed bubble of flatus produced by digestive juices attacking the foodstuffs of your latest meal, plus some of the air you've swallowed out of habit or nervousness. This bubble—composed of carbon dioxide, methane, and hydrogen—expands as you rise. Belching or breaking wind would make you more comfortable if you could bring it off. Underwater, that's not easy.

Most divers blame their pain on something they ate. They are one-third right. Two other causes are the air they swallow and the spontaneous cramping of sections of the colon without apparent cause or reason.

Most of us are habitual air swallowers. Air accumulates in the stomach with every bite we eat and every drop we drink. Excitement makes us swallow harder and faster.

The result can be a bolus of gas that rolls through the intestines along with more solid wastes. Most interior gas departs circumspectly without our knowing or helping. At times, it is trapped by a cramp that erects a muscular barricade.

Some foods seem automatically to produce excessive gas. Examples are beans, cabbage, cauliflower, and radishes. Milk is a gas-producing disaster for almost all blacks and many whites. Though they cannot metabolize its sugary content, many persist in drinking it because of its reputation as a perfect food.

Ill-considered habits can contribute to gas build-up in the stomach—swigging from a narrow-necked bottle, chewing with the mouth open, and gulping draughts of air that are returned through the larynx in explosive belches.

Prevention

First, refuse to eat those foods that are likely to gasify your digestive processes.

Second, stop any indecorous practices that introduce surplus air into your stomach. Even such seemingly innocent habits as chewing gum and sucking on jelly beans can provide the ingredients of a frightening gas ball inside your gut.

Third, review your consumption of milk and dairy products. If need be, give them up for a time to see if they might be causing an unexplained gas problem.

Fourth, follow each prediving meal with a serious effort to calm your nerves. Sometimes a short walk will do it, or just sitting for a spell in a rocking chair.

INFECTION

Infection is the invasion of the body by poisonous organisms and the reacton of the tissues to their presence. Any abrasion, wound, emotional shock, or the like provides an invitation for hordes of bacteria, protozoa, and helminths (parasitic worms) to storm one's vitals. They attack by land, sea, and air, riding dust and dirt particles, drops of water, and air currents. Wrestlers exchange them by the millions. A sneeze ten feet distant can send them hurtling onto your skin.

Doctors spend half their time fighting these single-celled, plant-like microorganisms. You must do the same if an injury is to heal without complications.

But first, you must determine if a wound is really infected. An oozing of clear yellowish fluid may look like pus when it actually is a healing serum that will turn quickly into a scab. Reddish wound lips are normal. The tissues are probably just pink from adjusting to the damage. If there's tenderness in adjacent areas, it's probably your lymph glands at work.

As a bacterial invasion begins to succeed, as microorganisms spread their poisons, your body will send out signals. Call them symptoms. For instance:

The wound will become hot. You will run a fever. (If above 101°, call your doctor.)

Red streaks may radiate outward from the site. The streaks are lymph channels that have become inflamed as a result of carrying away rotted tissue. In combination with other signals, they may indicate a greater or lesser degree of infection. Don't panic when you see them.

The site is tender and swollen, with festering (this happens after forty-eight to seventy-two hours). Sometimes, the wound will swell until it bursts, emitting pus. Self-healing may follow, but don't depend on it. Consult your physician.

Treatment

Mild soap and water are the best medicine. Any wound must be kept clean. If soiled clothing or adjacent skin areas press against it, lay on a sterile pad, taping it down. If the infection is advanced, a warm water soak with a soft pad, should be employed every three or four hours. One objective is to keep the scab soft and allow its self-healing process to finish the job. It will usually drop off in the second week of treament.

If the bacterial invaders succeed in counterattacking despite your best efforts, don't wait too long to call for help. Even physicians are not miracle men.

LOWER BACK PAIN

If you've never thought of lower back pain as a diver's malady, think again. It's everybody's malady. Only the common cold sends more people to doctors' offices. It probably costs vacationing divers more wasted days than all the pressure-related maladies combined.

Symptoms vary according to cause and degree of damage. You bend over and cannot straighten up. Pain blazes a hot line from the low back down a rear thigh, lodging sometimes in the knee, ankle, or big toe. The agony may keep you in bed or it may diminish to a dull ache.

Principal causes are *(1)* lifting heavy objects; *(2)* arthritic growths on the spine; and *(3)* a herniated spinal disc (commonly called a "slipped disc").

In lifting, there's a right way and a wrong way. The latter strains muscles about the base of the spine, causing a spasm that can double you up. Obviously, you asked your back muscles to do too much. The cure is usually bed rest, with cold packs for thirty-six hours, then hot applications. Prevention requires a stronger back and reborn abdominal muscles. And lifting the right way: Instead of bending over, reaching out, and lifting, get your legs beneath your center of gravity by keeping your spine in an upright position, or nearly so. To get low, bend the knees. When you lift, simply straighten the knees, lifting your upper body and your burden simultaneously.

Arthritic growths on the spine usually happen years after you've given up diving. Or lifting. Or enjoying life. In the wonderful world of drugs, your best bet for relief is the use of pain-killers.

Let's look at a herniated disc. As one observer has suggested, if you were to stack thirty-three spools onto each other and run a cord through them, you would have a fairly accurate model of a modern man's backbone, but lacking one important feature. In real life, each bony spool in the spine is separated from its neighbor by a doughnut-like pad of gristle about the size of a quarter. That pad is our culprit. The villain of America's most prodigious ache is a soft-centered, bouncy cushion with jelly in its middle, that we call a spinal disc. When it is crushed or damaged, we call it a slipped disc.

The truth is there's no such thing. Discs don't really slip; instead, they rip, wear, tear, break, crack, split, or rupture. And they hurt. The cause can be either wear and tear or a pinch. Or both. Age may be a factor. Middle-aged people seem to have more bad backs than youngsters.

Proper alignment of the vertebrae is important. Nerve fibers pass through tunnels in every vertebra. Low back nerve fibers carry messages from the brain to the legs. Any careless movement —a slip, fall, or twist— can grind a disc down until the rim bulges or breaks.

If it's a bulge, you are lucky. It may heal itself in two weeks. If it's a break that spills the pad's interior gel into the space around the nerve roots, you may be in for trouble. Pain will be intense, running down the leg. Numbness in a foot or toes may ensue. Severe lesions can produce paralysis.

Treatment

Apply cold compresses to the lower back. Rest. Put a bedboard under your mattress or sleep on the floor. Ten grains of aspirin or Tylenol every six hours will soothe. After thirty-six hours, switch to hot packs.

If there is no improvement, consult a doctor. He will surely order an X-ray called a myelogram. His reaction to what he sees in the picture may take you to the brink of a sticky bit of decision making. Many surgeons feel that the surest relief results only from a speedy operation. Often, they are wrong. Medical experience seems to indicate that nine times out of ten herniated discs are better left to heal without surgery.

Be a skeptic. Insist on another opinion, and maybe a third, until you are absolutely satisfied that your herniated disc can never be rested enough to repair itself.

You can prevent low back pain only if you keep your lumbar vertebrae lined up properly. Researchers have discovered that almost every person hurting from lower back pain suffers from an imbalance of the muscles serving the spinal column. Heavy hamstrings and strong gluteal muscles invariably overpower the quadriceps. A survey has showed average backside musculature to be ten to twelve times stronger than frontsides.

The remedy is to build up the front muscle structure with simple exercise drills. This will straighten the spine, balancing it to carry its load better. In doing so, first consider isometrics, the no-motion method that builds strength without moving a muscle.

Exercises

Sit or stand. Suck in your gut, pulling your navel back toward your spine with every ounce of strength in your abdominal muscles. Hold for a count of ten seconds. Relax.

Sitting or standing, contract your fanny muscles—the psoas— into the hardest, tightest knot you can make. Hold for a ten count. Relax.

Sitting or standing, suck your navel toward your spine with contracted abdominal muscles, and *at the same time* squeeze your rump into tight, twin balls of flesh. Hold for ten seconds. Relax.

Repeat this set of three movements whenever you think of it, at stop lights when are out driving, or while watching television. First you'll gain muscle tone, and presently you'll gain abdominal strength.

Add the following exercises and you'll make still faster progress.

The Knee Hugger. Repeat this exercise as often as possible.

1. Lie on your back. Bend the right knee, lifting it toward the chest. Grasp your leg with both hands and hug it to your chest. Hold for ten seconds, slowly drop the leg back to the floor while counting ten.
2. Repeat with the left leg.
3. Raise both legs at the same time, hug them to your chest as before, holding for a ten-count, and, slowly counting to ten, stretch out again.

The Spine Straightener. Here is another exercise to repeat until your abdominals begin to ache.

1. Lying relaxed and supine, slide your hand between your spine and the floor. Most individuals have a spinal curve that provides an inch or so of room. Your task is to flatten the spine and eliminate that space.
2. Make your abdominals pull your belly button toward the floor. Tighten your buttocks hard. Your pelvis will tip and your spine will straighten. Hold the position for ten seconds.

Some of us are too busy or too uncomfortable to lie down. Use a wall instead. Stand about six inches away from it. Lean back until your shoulders and butt make contact. Again, note the amount of space between the hollow of your back and the wall. You must eliminate that by flattening your spine against the wall. It's the previous floor exercise again, only you're standing up. Suck in your belly button. Tighten your butt hard. Tilt your pelvis. The space will vanish because your spine is straight. Relax. Repeat the drill every time you can manage it. You are training muscles long neglected. Don't be impatient.

The Curl. This drill should be used to augment earlier exercises. Lie on your back on the floor, knees bent and feet drawn up to rest about fourteen inches from the buttocks. Place the hands behind the neck. Flatten your spine against the floor. Begin the curl by slowly lifting the head, then the neck, and then your spine. Get the feeling that you are pulling your vertebrae, one at a time, away from the floor. Some people can lift all the way to a sitting position. Most of us with weak abdominals must start more modestly. We'll get the heavy head and neck clear, then the shoulders, and maybe a dozen of the thirty-three vertebrae. It's a good start. Hold the curl for a ten-count. Slowly uncurl to the original reclining position. Do this ten times a day.

Now you've got a measure of your abdominal strength. Finish every exercise session with a curl to see whether you are improving. Some experts will tell you to curl with your toes under a sofa or with a friend holding your feet down. Either is okay if it is only temporary. But it is better to do it unaided. Only when you can do it solo can you rely on your abdominal strength to keep you free of low back pain.

MUSCLE PULL

This affliction can send you either to your medicine kit for temporary relief or to the hospital. Hard to describe, it can turn a smooth-running hip into a gimpy joint. Divers usually pull muscles when they are training or climbing in or out of boats.

Why does it happen? Because your muscles are paired, with each member designed to pull against its opposite number. The thigh has its heavy quadriceps in front, its heavy hamstrings behind. The upper arm has its biceps in front, its triceps behind. When one muscle contracts with effort, the other muscle must relax. During a dive, this alternate contraction and relaxation happens hundreds or thousands of times. Untired muscles do it automatically. When tired muscles are driven by tired nerve cells, one member of a pair may fail to relax for a split-second. If that happens when the other muscle is flexing in a supreme effort, two muscles are pulling against each other. Something's got to give, and the weaker muscle tears. Books call the injury an "overstretching or rupture of a muscle or tendon." Pain usually hits unexpectedly. Suddenly, you are a cripple.

Treatment

What works for bruises works for muscle tears. Try to control the spread of subcutaneous bleeding by applying cracked ice in a plastic bag and compression bandages. Unless you gain control quickly, blood can perfuse tissues surrounding the injury and coagulate into a massive hematoma.

If the tear is close to the surface of the body, anticipate an early recovery. If it is deep, cancel your diving schedule, training schedule, and social activities. You need more than anything to rest the injury. Treat with cold compresses for the first thirty-six to forty-eight hours. Try to feel the tear's outline. When you are certain that the bleeding and spreading have stopped, administer heat. If the injury is deep, a doctor or a paramedic may have to use diathermy to break up the congestion.

Torn muscle fibers take time to heal. Total rest is your best ally. Gentle massage can smooth out kinks and warm the tissues. Eventually, try a very light workout. At first, the muscle will be tight. Continue with diathermy and moist heat. Retrain slowly.

Prevention of Recurrence

Always warm up for at least ten minutes, gently putting the injured muscle through the same arcs of action that are demanded by normal activity. When you are deeply tired from training exercises, swimming, diving, toting, whatever, never call on your body for a supreme effort.

NAUSEA AND MOTION SICKNESS

Some physical sensations cannot be described. Words simply won't tell the story of nausea, for instance. First, you turn yellow-pale. A film of clammy perspiration covers your body. Inevitably, there's vomiting. It happens to people on boats, in planes, and in scuba diving.

The cause is the movement of the juices inside the balancing apparatus in your inner ear (labyrinth). Eventually, your mixed-up sense receptors will adjust and you will be able to ride out surface actions and the currents they stir up under water. In the meantime, cope.

Treatment

If the water is choppy and you feel queasy, don't dive. Underwater vomiting is a disaster.

If you're on a dive boat, get your body horizontal as close to the boat's center of gravity as possible.

Fasten your eyes on a comparatively steady part of the vessel, avoiding peeks at the pitching horizon.

Don't try to read.

Stay on the windward side of sick people. Don't watch.

As a remedy, try sipping a cola or ginger ale. Fruit juices are sometimes refreshing. Or suck a piece of ice.

Prevention

Prepare yourself ahead of time. Don't overindulge in either alcohol or food. For most persons, skipping meals doesn't help. After eating, wait about three hours before you dive. Avoid gas-forming victuals like cabbage and beans. If the water's rough, protein is your best bet. Go easy on coffee.

Fighting nausea is a legitimate use for motion sickness pills. Drug stores sell them over the counter. Begin taking them two days before your expedition. Dramamine is the best known, and it is available around the world. But be careful—it induces severe drowsiness and disturbs coordination in some persons.

"Sure, sea-sickness has ruined many a diving day," a divemaster explains, "but if the water's that choppy, it's not fit for diving anyhow."

NOSE BLEED

You can get a nosebleed from diving, running into a limb, or bumping into your buddy's elbow. Underwater, a burst ear drum is often the cause, and the flow will be minimal. Regardless, if your nose is bleeding, you will want to stop it. Knowing the source helps. Most nosebleeds that flow enough to be a bother originate in the middle wall of the nose, that thin partition of bone and gristle called the septum. Its membrane covering is so tender that a blow can tear it. Usually, the flow is from only one nostril. If the source is high in the nose, however, blood may gush from both nostrils.

Treatment

First, sit down, which should reduce your blood pressure. If being semirecumbent is more comfortable, pile up diving gear or cushions and lean back on them, but keep the head erect in order to prevent blood from running into your throat. If it does, avoid swallowing the blood; it causes vomiting.

Place the forefingers of each hand below and on the outside of each nostril and press against the upper lip. (If you are helping another person, use your thumbs below the corners of *his* nose.) Press firmly but not enough to hurt. Maintain pressure for at least five minutes after which you may release it to see if the bleeding has ceased. If not, resume pressing on the upper lip for another five minutes. If three such pressure attempts do not stop the nosebleed, you should call a doctor.

Pressing with the fingers as described should have restricted the flow of blood to the bleeding point, thus giving blood cells at the site of the injury a chance to clot and form a plug. This happens to most people within five minutes. (Some physicians prescribe an initial pressure period of ten to fifteen minutes.)

An alternative technique is to grasp your nose between thumb and forefinger just below its hard upper part. Squeeze it firmly as if trying to shut out a bad odor.

Whichever method you use, once the bleeding has been stopped, roll up a firm, cigar-sized plug of cotton or sterile gauze, butter it with Vaseline, and push it into the leaky nostril until it presses against the bleeding site. Allow a tag of cotton or gauze to project from the nose to assist in its eventual removal. Keep this plug in place for three or more hours. When you do remove it, use great care, keeping in mind that a rough tug can start the nosebleed again.

Some experts warn amateurs against packing a nose, fearing the introduction of germs and its resultant complications. However, nurses have done it for years. If you choose to follow their example, make certain that your hands and your home-made nose plugs are sterile. Afterwards, remain quiet for several hours. Try not to talk, laugh, or cough.

SCIATICA

The sciatic nerve is the longest in the body. When it is inflamed, the pain can resemble a lighted fuse running beneath the skin from buttocks to big toe. Sometimes it stabs. Sometimes it smolders like a red hot wire. Sometimes it fades for hours or days only to return like a prairie fire.

The problem is a disturbance in the nerve root or thereabouts in your spine. Pressure does it. Or pulling. Or infection from a nearby organ.

Treatment

Refer to the section on low back pain.

SPRAINS AND STRAINS

Everybody has trouble remembering the difference between a sprain and a strain, including medical students.

A sprain is an injury to the joint.

A sprain involves the overstretching of the tough, fibrous cord (or cords) connecting one bone to another.

This connective cord is called a ligament.

A sprained joint involves a torn ligament and may include a slight fracture of the bone.

A strain is an injury to a muscle or to the tendon which attaches that muscle to a bone.

A strain involves an overstretching of a muscle and/or its attachment, with the result that some part of the muscle or its connection with the tendon or the bone is torn loose.

In sum, joints are sprained. Muscles are strained. Joints are held together by ligaments. Muscles are held to bone by tendons.

Sport divers rarely suffer sprains underwater. Topside, there seems to be no limit to them. One turns an ankle while carrying a dive bag, trips over a rock on a trail to a spring, or stumbles on a step. Scuba training programs offer a rich variety of opportunities. Since most sport divers are weekend athletes, there's usually no problem in predicting when they will suffer sprains. It will be on a weekend.

A sprain is no fun. Many orthopedic doctors consider it worse than a broken bone. If the initial sprain of any joint is not treated properly and allowed to heal fully, the joint is likely to succumb again and again to subsequent twist or tension.

Sprains are ranked as minor, in which ligaments may be stretched but not ruptured; moderate, in which the ligament is partially torn; or major, in which one or more ligaments are torn apart.

No cast is needed for a minor sprain. However, if the ligament is either partially or completely torn, a cast is obligatory. *The Complete Home Medical Encyclopedia* recommends this procedure:

> A walking cast is essential for six weeks (anything less will surely cause a recurrence). And after that the ankle is taped for two weeks. Next the ankle is treated to hot soakings. The patient must not engage in any sports or activities that would put a strain on the ankle for at least another three weeks, not until all stiffness and sensitivity have disappeared.

The total period of recuperation expected for a major sprain is about three months.

A *strain* is a slightly different injury. The *Emergency Medical Guide* describes it thus:

It is an overstretching of a muscle or a group of muscles in such a way that the little individual bundles making up the muscle are torn or the tendon by which the muscle is fastened to the bone which it moves, is stretched or ruptured.

A sudden, wrenching movement precipitates it; hence, the phrase, "I wrenched my back." So does lifting a scuba tank incorrectly.

Physicians usually classify strains into first, second, and third degrees of severity. A first-degree strain heals without complications. If a doctor speaks of your second or third degree strain, you can cancel your diving, skiing, or surfing expeditions until further notice. Torn muscle fibers are incapable of regenerating themselves. Fortunately, nature has arranged scar tissue to fill the gap and to hold the injured parts together. Scar tissue is inelastic, and its presence in a muscle reduces the latter's power of contraction. Therefore, a diver must not return to his sport until his injury is *totally* healed and the scar tissue that has grown into his muscles and tendons is linked so tenaciously into his living fibers that the healed spot will not come unstuck.

The time required for healing varies among individuals. A minor strain should heal in a fortnight. More serious strains can last for months, particularly in cases requiring surgical intervention.

Sprains occur most commonly at weight-bearing joints such as ankles, knees, hips, shoulders, elbows, wrists, fingers, and thumbs. *Strains* usually occur at or near muscular attachments to the bones they move. Inasmuch as most strains and sprains are similarly treated, we shall discuss them collectively, adding such other details as may be helpful in special situations. It is suggested that you read the following general information and then turn to the alphabetical list of injuries below before treating your own ailment.

General Treatment

Sprains and strains of all degrees may be treated conservatively in the beginning. Their progress in healing will dictate subsequent therapy.

Standard practice is to slow down the circulation of blood in injured tissue by the application of ice and compression bandages. Elevation of the part contributes to this end. Total rest is essential. After a strain or sprain has been iced a day or two, the application of heat (which may be diathermy) will warm up hard-to-reach muscles and help eliminate toxins. Limit massage to the muscles adjacent to the tear. Taping (by a professional) can be sought to protect against reinjury. Amateurish taping can do more harm than good. If mobility is essential, the brief use of crutches is advocated.

Sprained Ankles. Two types of sprained ankles are common. The first occurs when a foot is suddenly forced outward; the second when the foot is suddenly forced inward. About 85 percent of all sprains are on the outside. Their severity depends on the number of ligaments overstretched and the degree of tearing.

Three basic ligaments are involved in binding together the lower leg bone and your ankle bones. Nature has given you a neat, tight hinge with a solid junction firmly laced so that your foot can move freely only up or down, lifting the toes or depressing them.

In a mild sprain, the up-and-down movement of the foot causes little pain. Most soreness will be found in a dollar-size spot just in front of the outside ankle bone. If the area turns black, don't worry. A small blood vessel has probably been ruptured.

If the sprain is severe, the ankle will swell on both sides and be sore generally. If one cannot bear to move the foot upward or downward or put weight on it, a fracture is possible.

For a mild sprain, apply ice for twelve to thirty-six hours, wrap with a compression bandage, elevate, and rest the ankle for a few days.

For a moderate sprain, do the above but tape the ankle and treat it gently through the next few days. Recovery can be expected by the second or third week.

For a severe sprain, seek the advice of an orthopedic surgeon or better, a sports podiatrist. He will use X-rays. If the ankle is numb or deformed or too sore to touch, consider it an emergency and splint it gently with whatever is available: a wrap-around pillow will serve, or rolled-up newspapers. If possible, call for an ambulance, then ice and elevate the ankle. You need professional attention.

If the victim is forced to walk during the period before receiving professional help, reinforce the ankle with a necktie, belt, or bandage tied in a figure-eight about the joint. Remove it as soon as possible to encourage circulation. "If the pain doesn't go away, or if full function is not restored after 10 minutes, you should see a doctor," says Dr. Thomas D. Fahey, a sports physician.

Some trainers try to prevent reinjury by taping a recently injured ankle before every expedition or outing, and then packing it in ice for thirty minutes after the outing.

Finally, rehabilitation exercise must be used to limber up tight ligaments and new scar tissue. When you start heat treatments, wait one day and begin exercising. Simple flexions and dorsiflexions are enough at first. Pull your toes up (flexion), then point them down like a ballet dancer (dorsiflexion). Do this twice daily, twenty reps each time. After two days of limbering, try to evert the foot, raising the outer edge of the sole. Then roll it inward, putting the soles of both feet together. Do this twice daily as well, twenty reps each time.

Toe-raisers come next. Merely stand on tip-toe. Rise as far as you can, hold for a moment, and drop back onto your heels. Do a sequence of ten or twenty, then rest. Repeat several sequences in each session. Add additional toe-raisers (five or so per day) to the sequence as you are able. Eventually, you will be doing hundreds, the swelling will disappear, ankle soreness will become a memory, and your ginglimus joint (hinge) will have lost its rust and be as good as ever.

Calf strain. Anyone whose training program includes jogging or running is a candidate for calf strain. Symptoms are soreness, tightness, heat, swelling, sometimes discoloration from subsurface blood.

Tennis players occasionally suffer from a rupture in the belly of the gastronemius (calf) muscle. They call it "tennis leg;" and like most calf strains, it seems to be caused by a failure to get one's thick calf muscle stretched and warmed up in its interior.

Treatment is rest, ice packs, then heat and range of motion exercises such as toe-raisers and toe-pointers.

Prevention involves longer warm-up sessions and stronger lower leg muscles.

Hands. The hands are fragile creations of pipe-stem bones, loose tendons, and flimsy ligaments. They are good for clutching, grasping, and manipulating. As weapons, they are duds. Unless wrapped and pillowed within leather and tape, they collapse against any hard surface.

The thumb seems to be a special candidate for misery. We have the phrase, "sticking out like a sore thumb," a tribute to its frequency of being in the wrong place. If you jam a thumb, the odds favor a broken bone or a snapped ligament.

Only an X-ray can confirm a fracture. A self-test for ligament trouble is as follows: Place the tips of your thumb and forefinger together and pinch. If you've lost your pinching power, if there's pain but little squeeze left in your thumb, you've probably torn a ligament.

Doctors agree that if elevation, cold packs or ice, and compression for twenty-four hours do not cause the pain and swelling to subside, it's time to seek professional help.

Groin pull (strain or sprain). The groin is the depression where your lower abdomen joins either thigh. Several muscles cross this area. As a rule, they are not used much in sports and are therefore not well developed. Each of them is subject to the injury called groin pull.

Treatment of these out-of-the-way areas is a problem. After such an injury, some trainers recommend that all exercise be discontinued until it has healed. Others advocate icing for early healing and taping or bandaging during the last stages.

Preventive measures are limited to mild stretching exercises during the healing period and later as a permanent addition to one's weekly routine.

Dr. Thomas D. Fahey recommends these groin stretchers:

1. Sit on floor. Draw your feet toward the buttocks and place the heels together. Separate the knees so they are *outside* the arms. Push down gently on the thighs with the elbows, further separating the knees and stretching the tissues in the groin. Hold for ten seconds and relax. Repeat.

2. Sit on floor with straight legs, feet wide apart. Place the hands on the floor between the legs and lean forward at the hips feeling the stretch in your hamstrings and groin. Later, as you become more flexible, move the feet farther apart to the utmost unpainful limit. Hold each stretch for ten seconds and relax. Repeat a half-dozen times.

3. From an erect position, place one foot forward with a bent knee while extending the other leg backward in the classic thrust position. Lean over the forward leg, with your hands touching the floor for balance, until you feel a stretching sensation in the groin area.

Note: Remember that overstretching can be hazardous. Make each stretching session brief, controlled, and only strenuous enough to produce a slight lengthening of your tight groin muscles. Eventually, the groin pull will heal itself and the muscles will be much stronger.

Knee sprains and strains. The human knee must be the most vulnerable of all joints. Certainly, it is the most publicized. The knees of Mickey Mantle, Joe Namath, and others have been headlined through two generations. The knee is so complicated that books have been written to explain its workings. We recommend Chapter 11 of *The Complete Book of Sports Medicine,* by Richard H. Domingues, M.D., published by Charles Scribner's Sons.

Scuba diving is singularly free of knee problems. The flutter kick favored by most divers is easy on knee muscles, ligaments, and tendons. The only divers who seem to have problems are former competitive breast-strokers. Modern breast-stroking calls for a whip kick that explodes behind, producing speed. In turn, this action calls for the leg to be turned outward from the knee down. This puts stress on the knee's inner surface. Eventually, it wears or tears knee tissues and creates a malady called "breast-stroker's knee."

Breast-strokers who have become scuba divers and use the whip kick have promptly given it up. They don't need it. Speed comes from their flippers and streamlining. For those who do feel a strain on their knees, the answer is simple. Take it easy, start a conditioning program to build up your quadriceps, and learn the flutter.

Lower back sprain. The lower back is the area that rises from the rear of the pelvis to the lowermost ribs. Its injury involves both muscles and ligaments and results from a blow, a slip, a pull, or a fall in which the lower back is twisted or forcefully bent backward beyond its normal range of motion. Although pain may be deferred, it is usually felt immediately. Stiffness develops with swelling.

Treatment calls for the immediate application of cold packs or ice and compression bandaging. Repeat the cold applications every two hours the first day. Rest on a hard mattress. Don't try to walk through pain. On the second day after the injury, and no sooner, apply heat and gradually initiate a program of gentle stretching exercises.

Sometimes a back sprain will pinch a nerve, in which case you may feel a darting pain down one leg. That is the sciatic nerve complaining. A herniated disc is usually responsible, calling for a visit to the doctor. If you want to tough it out, go to the drug store and order a Boston brace. It is particularly effectve at straightening out an excessive spinal curve.

Among Americans, lower back muscles are notoriously weak. The best defense against lower back sprain is the development of muscles strong enough to withstand the buffetings of your lifestyle. Lower back exercises, thrice weekly or more, will generally produce a pain-free back. (See "Low Back Pain".)

Shoulders. The shoulder is a complicated, troublesome, invaluable set of joints, muscles, tendons, and ligaments too sophisticated to treat in this brief space. Actually, it is three joints in one, all working together to provide arm motion in any direction. The main joint consists of a half-dollar size socket into which a bony ball (the head of the humerus) is bound by a tangle of fibroid cords. Things can go wrong tendon by tendon or in painful concert. Shoulder muscles can speed a baseball faster than 100 miles per hour. Most divers go a lifetime, however, without suffering a shoulder injury.

Swimmer's shoulder is an injury that new divers sometimes bring to the sport. Actually, it is the result of overuse plus sprain or strain. Teenagers experience it after such illnesses as colds, flu, and mononucleosis. Seasoned adults using certain strokes move their arms in a way that reduces the flow of blood to tendons. Lack of oxygen and nutriment causes a build-up of metabolites (debris) in the cells which swell and hurt. Distance freestylers, backstrokers and butterfliers are most often affected.

Because symptoms are almost identical with those of tendonitis, most physicians who do not work regularly with athletes recommend treatment for that affliction and the total discontinuance of swimming until healing has occured. An alternative most divers use is to ask for a second opinion. Or to try a change in their stroke mechanics—it can make a big difference. Ice massage before and after a swim is generally pain-reducing.

Because so little shoulder strain is experienced in scuba work, many lame-shouldered snorkelers have abandoned surface diving and joined the air tank brigade long enough to rest their fatigued joints. Reports indicate that it works.

Miscellaneous sprains and strains. Because anybody can fall on his shoulder, wrenching tendons and ligaments, it should be understood that the faithful formula of cold packs and compression is the way to begin any first aid effort. Follow it up after a day or two with plenty of heat. One trainer of note simply removes a shower head and directs a powerful stream of hot water full force at the site of an injury. Reportedly, this hydrotherapy is successful.

Coincidentally, after the shoulder is warmed through, begin range-of-motion exercises. As soon as full range is attained, shift gradually to weight conditioning to strengthen the muscles and provide a new and better junction of the lattice-work of shoulder tendons and ligaments that assures proper functioning.

Toe sprain. Stubbed toes rank near the top of any list of aquatic injuries. There is no accounting for bare-footed mankind's awkwardness either above or below the water's surface.

What to do? If the injury seems bearable, soak the foot in cold water for an hour or so. Next, immobilize the toe by taping it to its nearest larger neighbor. Elevate it. Make certain that the taping is loose enough to permit some swelling.

Next day, apply hot soaks (about 90 degrees) or whirlpool treatments of ten minutes each, twice daily. Gentle massage is useful, if applied above and below the site of injury, never directly on it, twice a day for five minutes.

If the injury is severe, a physician should examine it (X-ray) for a fracture. All the above measures should be taken as soon as possible after the accident. Cold water therapy can be extended through the second or third day. Wrap the foot in an elastic bandage to moderate swelling. Keep it elevated above the level of the heart. Rest.

In a serious strain, apply heat only after swelling abates, and then soak the foot in water heated to 90 to 100 degrees three times daily. If the swelling continues, alternate hot and cold soaks. Rest as much as possible. If you must walk regardless of the need for rest, wrap the toe in an analgesic balm pack.

If the little toe is crippled, tape it to its companion so that it has support. If the big toe is hurt, you can relieve the pressure on it by taping it to a thin strip of wood an inch deep and as wide as your foot. Place it so that it supports the forward portion of the ball of the foot, which is just ahead of the widest part of the shoe. This will raise the forefoot with every step, relieving it of bearing weight and making your walk almost comfortable.

Hamstring pulls (or muscle-and-tendon ruptures). The hamstring, which is really a group of several muscles, lies beneath the thighbone (if one is sitting). When it ruptures seriously, you usually know it because it makes a loud pop. Coaches say it is one of the most frequent injuries suffered by athletes. Swimmers are usually spared this injury unless they are also competitive sprinters.

Pulls happen because of an imbalance between the right and left leg and also because of the hamstring's weakness compared to the strength of the thicker muscle atop the thighbone, the quadriceps. Studies have shown that a pull will happen if one hamstring is more powerful than the other by 10 percent or more. Also, that the hamstring must be at least two-thirds as strong as the quadriceps of the same leg. In other words, if your quadriceps can lift ninety pounds (on a leg-lift machine), its matching hamstring must be able to lift sixty pounds.

Other factors that contribute to tears and strains are speed-work in cold weather and inadequate warm-up at any temperature.

Whether tears are slight or severe, the initial treatment is cold packs and compression bandages. Continue for twenty-four hours in a mild case; Forty-eight to seventy-two if severe. Minor tears frequently are not noticed until an hour or so after exercise. Serious tears announce themselves immediately; the runner hears or feels the rupture. In the latter case, professional help is essential.

A major tear heals slowly, often taking months. Victims must be patient and remember that they will never be quite as strong at the point of injury as they were. Also, the scar tissue in their hamstrings is a little more liable to pop again than was the original tissue. And finally, the prevention of their next tear requires a steady ten to fifteen minute warm-up, in addition to the balancing of thigh strengths both from side to side and from fore to aft.

Wrist sprain. Will the diver who has never suffered a sprained wrist please stand up? You're coming out of the surf, tanks on your shoulders, a flipper catches on a rock as a wave recedes. Over you go, catching your weight on your hands. It also happens on docks, decks, even golf greens. Result—a sprained wrist!

Many doctors say it is the most poorly managed injury in sports, which is why you should know more about it. First, a large chunk of your brain is devoted to the wrist and hand unit because it is the instrument through which you learn so much. Even with your eyes closed, the hand tells you about surface texture, size, weight, shape, hardness, or temperature.

Taking care of the wrist isn't easy. Seven wrist bones and a half-dozen muscles are involved, not to mention the network of ligaments, tendons, nerves, and blood vessels that tie the package together. A spill is a serious matter.

Treatment begins with cold applications, ice packs, or immersion of the wrist in ice water. Because a wrist fracture and a wrist sprain look alike, some trainers automatically observe this rule: if the pain does not subside after ten minutes, go to the doctor for an X-ray.

A useful diagnostic trick is to bend the wrist back pointing the fingers upward. If this movement is impossible or excruciatingly painful, a bone is probably broken. Splint the wrist to prevent movement and get to a physician.

If there is no break, standard first aid treatment is to continue cold packs for twenty-four hours with a compression bandage and elevation. Next day, switch to heat packs. After applying heat, commence range-of-motion exercises. You can do this by yourself, limbering the tender wrist with your other hand, flexing it in all four directions, and finally rotating it.

Future protection depends on developing stronger wrist muscles.

Isometric wrist exercises. Note: The isometric principle of exercise requires that muscles be contracted but that their length remain the same. Example: place your hands together before your chest, as if in prayer. Gradually push the hands together until each arm is pushing with full force against the other. Hand, arm, and shoulder muscles will be fully tensed; but they will not change their length as happens in isotonic exercise. Research has shown that all-out contraction held for six to ten seconds promotes both muscle cell growth and an increase in strength.

1. Sit with your right side to a table, right elbow on it, the wrist at the edge. Let the hand hang over the edge. Place the left hand against the back of the dangling hand. As you try to straighten the injured wrist, hold it immobilized (in the downward position) by resisting with the left hand for ten seconds. Rest and repeat ten times.

2. Assume the same position with the injured wrist bending the hand upward pointing the fingers at the ceiling. With the left hand pressing hard against the back of the raised hand as if to straighten the wrist, resist movement for ten seconds. Rest and repeat ten times.

3. In a sitting position, clasp your hands together vertically with fingers interlaced so the right thumb, is on top. Hold the hands comfortably and bend them upward at the wrists. You will use the right wrist and arm muscles to maintain that bent-up attitude. You will use the left wrist and arm muscles to try to straighten the right wrist. When ready, clasp hands firmly together and gradually increase the opposing forces. If the injured wrist hurts, stop. If no pain ensues, increase pressure to full strength. Hold ten seconds and relax. Repeat the maneuver ten times.

4. Clasp hands as before, but interlace the fingers with the left thumb on top. This time, bend the hands *downward*. Now, you will oppose the left hand's up-twisting action by opposing it with the set muscles of the right wrist and arm. Stop if you feel pain. Continue all out if you can. Relax and repeat ten times.

5. For flexibility, make a "wrist machine." You'll need two feet of broom handle, five feet of Venetian blind cord, and a five-pound weight (or a five-pound bucket of bricks). Fasten the weight to one end of the cord, the broomstick to the other. With the weight on the floor, grasp each end of the stick, stand erect, and wind the rope up on the stick until the weight is hip high. Unwind and repeat. Continue until the wrists

tire. Go through a dozen wind-and-rest sets each day. As your wrists improve, add more bricks to the bucket (or use heavier weights). You have now exercised the wrists in four planes using isometic and isotonic exercises. Continue these exercises daily. Eventually, the wrists will regain their old mobility and protect you with improved muscle tone as well as enhanced strength.

SUNBURN

Maybe you are a heliophobe and don't know it. A heliophobe takes a short, sunny swim and comes out of the water as red as a beet. Depending on the time of day and length of exposure, his skin may turn pink, itch that night, blister the next day, and peel twenty-four hours later. And how it burns! What a way to start a vacation.

Heliophobe or not, understanding the problem may help you to avoid a painful sunburn.

Skin is a three-ply miracle. It is waterproof, bug-proof, and germ-proof. Only stinging, pricking invaders (e.g., mosquitos, sea urchins) can easily penetrate it.

Living skin's outer ply is composed mostly of dead and dying cells. If it were harder, one would call it *horn*. Its technical name is *epidermis*. Its dead cells drop off, rub off, and pop off constantly, to be replaced from the layers below.

The skin's manufacturing facilities are spread through a thick underlayer called the dermis. This structure houses millions of hair follicles, sweat and oil glands, nerves, and blood vessels. Cells work here day and night, reproducing and repairing.

Between the epidermis and dermis lies another layer—frail, specialized, and very color-conscious. These billions of working cells are called melanocytes and their function is to protect people from solar radiation.

How do they do it?

To oversimplify, they create a sheath of living cells that blocks the sun's ultraviolet rays. They are like sunscreens, like the window shades in your house, and they are responsible for the process we call getting a tan. When we abuse the mechanism or don't know about it, we call the result getting sunburned.

If you give the melanocytes a fair shake, like fifteen minutes a day exposure to the sun for the first three days, you've got a chance of peaking into a safe tan in about three weeks.

If you try to hurry the process, you may stir up a poisonous brew in your tissues. Too much ultraviolet radiation penetrating the body releases a chemical (archidonic acid) that is an irritant. The inflammation it produces is sunburn. Long range, those same rays do permanent damage to the skin's elastic fibers so that they cannot regenerate themselves. Saying it another way, the elastic fibers that keep cheeks smooth and skin taut lose their bounce under the sun. The result, say authorities, is premature wrinkling.

Treatment

When your skin is fiery hot from too much sun, you must take countermeasures. First, take a double dose of aspirin. Repeat after four hours. If your usual dose for a headache is ten grains, take twenty; if only five grains, take ten. Then cut back to normal. This reduces the pain and is a move toward controlling inflammation. Next, get into a bathtub full of cold water. Remain there as long as the skin feels hot.

Or skip the cold bath in favor of a mixture of oil and ice and water. Fill a basin with one pint of vegetable or bath oil (bath oil smells better), a gallon of water, and enough cracked ice to drop the temperature below seventy degrees. Saturate a towel and lay it on your burned skin.

If blisters develop, leave them alone. The aim is to prevent infection. Even a needle-hole in the skin can admit an army of germs. You've got a second degree burn, so treat it accordingly. (See "Burns.")

Any number of over-the-counter and prescription drugs are available for the final stages of healing. Some of the favorites are Noxzema, Solarcaine, Unburn, Unguentine Spray, Americaine, or Medicone Creme. A good pharmacist knows what works effectively and safely.

Prevention

Stay out of the midday sun. Midday for a sunbather is from eleven A.M. to three P.M. Never trust a beach umbrella. Sand and water can reflect damaging rays under it. A cloudy sky is often no better, for studies show that even an unbroken overcast permits four-fifths of the sun's damaging rays to pass through.

If you're in diving gear, don't fool around topside. Divers within three feet of the surface might as well be in a fireless cooker.

Tender-skinned snorkelers will have special problems with water droplets and greasy lotions. The drops sit up like tiny magnifying lenses on the skin and concentrate the sun's rays into painful blister clusters.

When in the sun, use a chemical sunscreen. The medical profession agrees that the best protection offered thus far is PABA, a unique kind of acid that blocks most ultraviolet rays. Better yet for some people is PABA-plus-zinc-oxide which is trademarked RVPaque. It blocks rays wholesale and sticks to your skin no matter how much you sweat. If you use it, you'll get no burn, no blisters—and probably no tan.

If you must have a tan, and you do want to protect your skin, the ultimate solution may be a cautious first three days in the sun with only fifteen minutes of exposure during each of those days. Later, increase exposure moderately day by day. In about three weeks, you will have a satisfactory tan.

If time is short (or self-control difficult) and you are using chemical screens and blockers, remember that most of them wash away with every dive. Carry extra prevention in your dive bag.

SWELLING

What actually is swelling?

One theory holds that it is nature's method of persuading impulsive, impatient human beings to lay back for a while. It gives the healing fluids in their bodies a chance to repair hurts that come between them and their immediate goals. Drop a tank on a toe; it will swell. Bump into a motel door, slip on a dock, turn an ankle, catch a finger in a van door. Swellings are a dime a dozen.

Athletes don't like them because they constrict the movement of joints, forcing the postponement of dives, games, and holidays. Trainers and physicians usually try to reduce swellings as quickly as possible.

In a way of speaking, a swelling is nature's splint, designed to keep the injured out of more serious trouble. Start with this basic truth: nearly every injury suffered in a sports activity will be followed by swelling. Body cells are served by thread-like vessels called capillaries that distribute blood and pick up lactic acid and other by-products of metabolism. When an injury occurs, thousands of those capillaries are smashed, ruptured, or torn. Blood oozes from them and invades adjacent cells. Plasma drains into every unfilled space, hardening the area. As swelling progresses, stiffening of the area accompanies it, preventing function. That is exactly what a good splint does.

In order to reduce or prevent swelling, you must take evasive action.

First, elevate the part. Raise an injured leg to a level higher than the heart. Prop a foot on a pillow. Lay a wrist on a shoulder-high chairback or shelf or pile of books on a table. If you've bumped your head badly, don't lie down. That would double the pressure in your capillaries and force more and more liquid into the injured flesh.

Second, apply external pressure to control the swelling. Soft flesh can be stretched from within into amazing bulges. A wrap-around elastic bandage provides the outside counterpressure needed to hold the injured tissues together. Take care that the wrapping imposes its greatest pressure directly over the injury site, while looser wraps at each end leave blood free to enter and exit from the disaster area.

Third, use cold applications for two days at least. Some trainers believe these are not worth the trouble. They may help; they cannot hurt. Cold slows down one's circulation; and in most injuries, this is what you want.

On the third day, if complications have not developed, try moderate heat. Wet packs, changed every fifteen minutes or so. Heat will not reduce a swelling, but it may liberate some of the stiffened flesh around the injury's perimeter. Psychologically, it also pacifies the spirit and tranquilizes the mind. Most of all, exploit the healing power of rest.

A word of warning concerning swellings that appear spontaneously: If you cannot recall a bump or fall or collision that might be the cause, an internal organ's failure may be responsible. Consult a doctor. The trouble could stem from the heart, kidney, liver, a blood clot, or some other source. Scientific tests will tell you what to do next.

INGROWN TOENAILS

Your big toe—or any toe—becomes sore. You discover that one corner of its nail is digging into adjacent flesh. The skin where the nail disappears is almost scarlet, hot, and tender to the touch.

Look at your thumb. The corners are rounded off and curve painlessly into a groove of flesh on each side that runs to the nail's base with its white half-moon. No pain, no inflammation there because there's no pressure on those rounded corners. The foot is different. It is usually encased in tight shoes and unforgiving socks and hammered at every step by your body's weight. So the nail's edge begins to jab and cut.

Treatment

You need to get the toenail's cutting edge out the groove of tender flesh.

Soak your foot in warm water for twenty minutes to soften the toenail and make it easier to handle. Use the wooden end of a Q-tip (pare it down if it is too stubby) to lift the toenail upward. Run this wooden wedge under the top margin of the toe, moving it toward the tender spot, lifting the nail gently until it is clear of the groove of inflamed flesh.

Dust the site with an antiseptic powder. Next, take a wisp of cotton (a fold of toilet paper will do in a crisis) and pack it carefully beneath the nail's edge so that it holds the nail up from the painful groove.

Repeat this procedure each morning until the point of the nail has grown beyond the groove from which you pried it. If you've been careful and no infection has set in, it should heal satisfactorily.

Prevention

Most of us round off our fingernails when we trim them. When we first trim our toenails, some of us do the same thing. But toenails must be cut *straight across*. Leave the corners *on* and out of the groove. That way, as they grow they cannot gouge.

UNCONSCIOUSNESS

Dr. John Henderson says, "One of the most baffling situations requiring emergency care is the unconscious person." People become unconscious for many reasons, from drug overdoses to diabetes. Sport divers become unconscious for special reasons such as asphyxia, shallow water blackout, hypoxia, or air embolism.

In any case, the condition presents an emergency that needs immediate attention. What caused it? Skin color is a clue. If it is pale white, the cause may be heat exhaustion, hemorrhage, shock, heart attack, or stroke. If it is blue, the victim probably is suffocating from lack of oxygen. He may have been shocked by contact with a live wire or throttled by a rope around his neck. He may have choked on a piece of steak. If the skin is red, the cause may be sunstroke, concussion, or a fractured skull.

Always look elsewhere for corroboration. Drunkenness also results in unconsciousness. The skin of a passed-out drunk can be red, white, or blue.

Fainting often looks like unconsciousness. But leveling the

fainted victim, with the feet higher than the head usually results in revival within a few minutes.

Treatment

Keep the patient quiet.

Look for bodily injuries, bleeding, broken bones, a blocked airway.

Lay the victim on his back; and if the face is pale, raise the legs. If the face is flushed, raise the head and shoulders.

Look for a medical identification disk on wrist or neck or in a billfold. You may have a diabetic on your hands, and the disk may indicate your next move. If he's diabetic, the cause is probably either insulin shock (lack of sugar in the blood) or diabetic coma (excess sugar). The latter causes the skin to turn red, feverish, and dry; the former, a white, wet skin.

Check the pulse. If there is none, start external heart massage.

Check the breathing. If the chest fails to rise and fall rhythmically, clear the airway and start artificial respiration.

If internal injury is suspected, the nose, mouth, or ears may be bleeding, or emitting a pale, straw-colored liquid. Either exudate usually denotes a serious injury that a doctor should know about fast.

Some first-aiders break an ampule of ammonia and wave it under the victim's nose. Recent doctrine advises against it, leaving that chore to a physician.

Remember that unconsciousness is a symptom, not a disease. Diagnosing its origin is no job for amateurs. Call for professional help at the first possible moment.

If the victim must be moved, lift the body so that the entire spinal cord is protected from twisting or bending. Vertebrae might be fractured. Ten hands are barely enough; four on each side and two under the head and neck.

UNDERWATER BLACKOUT

This is not a disease; it is a condition. Man's breathing satisfies two needs. Inhaling, he fills his lungs with oxygen. Exhaling, he empties his lungs of the gaseous waste carbon dioxide (CO_2). On orders from the brain, chest muscles contract and lift the rib cage, creating a vacuum into which fresh air pours. Relaxing muscles drop the rib cage, forcing out waste gases.

The trigger for every inhalation is in one's brain. Nature has assembled a clump of specialized brain cells to supervise breathing. These cells send their ceaseless orders via the nervous system. The agent that commands them to act is the carbon dioxide dissolved in one's blood. When CO_2 reaches a certain arterial concentration, the brain's order goes out: breathe!

Early divers tried breathing through reeds and carrying air in bladders. Eventually they learned that a dozen deep breaths before submerging increased their bottom time. The knowledge spread to pearl divers, treasure hunters, and snorkel divers. A good many drowned for no apparent reason. Modern science has learned why: Overbreathing uncocks the trigger (carbon dioxide) that normally orders the next breath. During the extra time gained on the bottom, one's cells continue to gobble up what remains of the oxygen in the blood. Anoxia hits the brain, numbing it before it recognizes its danger. Seconds later, it blacks out.

Treatment

Get the victim to the surface. Apply artificial respiration.

Prevention

Don't breathe deeply more than a half-dozen times before diving. Don't try to break breath-holding records. People vary greatly in their sensitively to CO_2. Discover your own tolerance and don't press your luck.

WARTS

Nobody wants them, everybody gets them, old and young. Divers are no exceptions. A wart under a fin or face mask or on the sole of the foot can spoil a dive and deserves attention.

Warts come in many sizes and species. Everyone recognizes the common, cauliflower-like bud that grows on hands, fingers, feet, or neck. Rough-surfaced, yellow in color, horny, it often hangs on for months.

There are other warts, equally troublesome. Worst is the plantar wart, a growth that is flattened by foot pressure and, because it cannot grow outward, grows inward and upward through the foot until it cripples. There is also the filiform wart, a small, thread-like outgrowth on the eyelids, face, and neck. And the flat wart, so-named because it lies flat on the skin, is tannish, yellowish, or sometimes brown. All are a temptation to fingers that want to pick and pluck. All are nuisances and should be treated with respect. The safest practice in dealing with them is to consult a physician or specialist.

WOUNDS

Pollution of water and air increases daily. Any break in a diver's skin can open the door to a host of bacteria. Bacteria are like people; they come in families, tribes, and clans. They are too small to see with the naked eye and are so tiny that thirty trillion of them weigh only one ounce. Over the centuries, they have adapted to almost every condition of life. Some prosper in cold weather. Some can live only in hot water. Some settle like colonies of senior citizens; others have whip-tails that bounce them around. Some bacteria are useful. Some are killers.

Fortunately, most wounds can be treated effectively from a diver's emergency medical supplies. A clean wound will heal. A dirty wound will get worse before it gets better. If the injury is unclean, within a week after the injury it will turn red, feel feverish, and become tender to the touch. Nearby lymph glands in the groin, armpit, or neck may hurt and look swollen.

Treatment

Large wounds bleed a lot, and the loss of blood is always a threat. Treatment for them starts with stopping the flow. (See "Bleeding".) Resolute pressure on the injury site usually does it.

If bleeding continues, place 4 × 4 gauze bandages over the wound and maintain pressure for ten minutes to give the blood time to coagulate.

Place the patient in a horizontal position or close to it. If possible, the wound should be above the level of the heart.

What if you have a puncture wound that doesn't bleed? What if it is hemorrhaging under the skin, only seeping or oozing on the surface? Watch it! The blood vessels could have gone into spasm. If that's the case, when they relax, blood will flow freely.

When the flow is stanched, clean the area with soap and water. Direct scrubbing strokes away from the wound, sweeping foreign matter off and not into the injury. If clean water is scarce and hydrogen peroxide is available, wet some pads with it and soak the injury for at least five minutes.

For a final clean-up, wipe the area with an alcohol-base drying antiseptic such as Betadine. You'll get about the same result with a salt water application (one-half teaspoon of salt in eight ounces of water). What about the old reliables, iodine and mercurochrome? Because they sometimes damage tissue, the new breed of first aiders say they are dangerous. Even leaving a layer of soapy water on the wound is preferable. Take your choice.

Finally, dress the wound. Use a sterile gauze pad that comes in a sealed envelope. Be careful not to touch its surface with your fingers. Spread an antiseptic ointment on the pad, not on the wound. A favored OTC dressing is Neosporin, the trade name for bacitracin. This is a powerful drug that makes a clean sweep of local surface bacteria without invading adjacent tissues and affecting their functions. Fix the pad in place with tape or a bandage.

Change the dressing according to the wound's general appearance of cleanliness and health. If it continues to bleed, tidy it up a lot. With each new bandage, apply a fresh coat of ointment.

If the wound is painful, deep, or ragged and hard to clean, get a tetanus shot. Don't put this off for more than forty-eight to sixty hours. Healing begins down deep and progresses to the surface. Examine the wound occasionally. Check it for redness. Feel it for hotness. Palpate it gently for infection. If pus bubbles up, get to a physician promptly.

Index

abrasions, 86-87
acetaminophen, 110, 121
air, 60-62, 66-67; components of,
    61. *See also* compressed air
air embolism, 68-70
air pressure, 62-63
air sacs, 61, 62
alcohol, 88-89
aloe plant, 101-102
aluminum chloride, 91
alveoli, 61
American Medical Association,
    111
American Standards Committee
    on Underwater Safety, 23;
    swimming test, 23
amphetamines, 109
ankles, 42-44
anoxia, 89, 152
anticongestants, 81-82
arteries, 12, 19; carotid, 29-30
ascent. *See* emergency ascent
aspirin, 110, 121, 147
asthma, 89-90
athletes foot, 90-93
axons, 15-16, 17-18

bacitracin, 154
backpacker's palsy, 93
bandages, 87
Barber, Jerry, 41
barotraumas, 64, 65
Bassler, Tom, 88
beer, 88
bends. *See* decompression
    sickness
benedryl, 116

blackout, underwater, 151-152
bleeding, 93-95, 118, 119, 153
blisters, 95-97
blood, 10-12, 18-21
bones, 12
boric acid, 92
Bowerman, William, 56, 58
Bowerman-Harris program, 57-59
brain, 16-17
bronchi, 61
bronchioles, 61
bruises, 97-100; back, 98-99; but-
    tocks, 99; fingernail, 100; hip,
    99; lower leg, 99; thigh, 99
burns, 100-102; first degree, 100,
    101; second degree, 100, 101-
    102; third degree, 100, 102
Burpee Thrust, 33-34

caffeine, 109
calf strain, 139
calluses, 102-104
capillaries, 12, 19, 65
carbon dioxide, 61-62, 70-71, 117,
    152
carbon dioxide poisoning, 70-71
carbon monoxide poisoning, 71-73
Castellani Paint, 91
Catlett, G. F., 108
certification, 22
chafing, 104-105
charley horse, 99, 105-106
chiggers, 106-107
chilling, 112
chocolate bars, 109
circadian dysrhythymia. *See* jet
    lag

circadian rhythms, 107-108
circuit training, 55
circulation, 18, 21
clotting, 95
cocoa, 109
coffee, 108-109
cola drinks, 109
colds, 110-11
cold water, 112-13, 123-24
Complete Book of Sports Medicine, The, 140
compressed air, 63, 66; efficient use of, 66-67
conditioning exercises, 55-59
Coolidge, Calvin, Jr., 96
Cooper, Donald, 117
Cooper, Kenneth H., 37
Cooper test, 37
coral, 113-14
coral poisoning, 114
Counsilman, James E., 40
Cousteau, Jacques, 6
Craig and Dehn, 24
cramps, 114-17
cuts, 117-20; in the mouth, 119; on brow, 120; on chin, 120; on eye, *see* eye cuts; on face, 119-20; on lips, 119; on scalp, 120; on tongue, 119

decompression, 73, 78
decompression sickness, 70, 73-75, 82
decompression tables, 73-74, 82
decongestants, 111, 121
deltoid muscle, 49
Demont, Rick, 89-90
dendrites, 16
diaphragm, 20
discs, herniated, 129-30, 141
Domingues, Richard H., 140
Drury, Francis, 40

ear, foreign object in, 121; inner, *see* inner ear
earache, 120-21
eardrum, ruptured, 65
ear plugs, 122, 123
emergency ascent, 75-77; suggestions for, 76

endurance, 53-54; conditioning for, 54
epidermophytosis, 90-93
Eustachian tube, 65, 80-82, 110, 111, 121
exhaustion, from cold water, 123-24; from heat, 126; from over-exertion, 124
extensors, 39
eye cuts, 12, 124
eyes, foreign bodies in, 125

Fahey, Thomas E., 138, 140
first aid, 85-86
flexors, 39
foot baths, 102

gas, intestinal, 126-27
Golding, Lawrence, 31
grusefulvin, 93
groin pull, 140

hamstrings, 45-46, 143
hamstring pulls, 143-44
Harris, W. E., 56, 58
heart, 18-20
heat exhaustion, 126
hematomas, 98, 132
Henderson, John, 150
hood squeeze, 77
hypothermia, 112
hypoxia, 89

Ikehara, Akim J., 2-3
infection, 88, 102, 114, 118, 127-28; of ear, 120-21
ingrown toenails, 149-50
inner ear, 64-65
interstitial emphysema squeeze, 77-78
intertigo. *See* chafing
interval training, 55-56
intestinal gas, 126-27
isometric exercises
    ankle strengthener no. 1, 43
    for wrist, 144-46
    frog leg hang, 50-51

hamstring strengthener no. 1, 46

hamstring strengthener no. 2, 46-47

hamstring strengthener no. 3, 47

knee strengthener no. 1, 44

knee strengthener no. 2, 44-45

knee strengthener no. 3, 45

shoulder strengthener series no. 1, 48-49

shoulder strengthener series no. 2, 49

shoulder strengthener series no. 3, 49-50

tiger stretch, 51

toe pointer no. 1, 42

toe pointer no. 2, 42-43

toe pointer no. 3, 43-44

isometrics, 38-40; examples of, 41; principles of, 40-41, 144-45

jet lag, 107-108
jogging, 54, 56-57

Kiphuth, Bob, 110
knee sprains and strains, 140-41

Lamb, Lawrence E., 90, 109, 110
Lanphier, Edward H., 27
leucocytes, 10-11, 96
ligaments, 136, 138
lower back pain, 128-30; exercises to prevent, 130-32
lower back sprain, 141
lungs, 61
lung squeeze, 78-79

mask squeeze, 79-80
mediastinal emphysema, 80
mediastinum, 80
Merck Manual, The, 25
middle ear squeeze, 80-82
Mirkin, Gabe, 87
Modern Medicine, 108
Morton's foot, 104
motion sickness, 133-34
Mount, Tom, 2-3

Muller and Hettinger, 40
muscle-and-tendon rupture, 143-44
muscle pull, 132-33
muscles, 13-14; function of, 39
muscle tone, 14

NASDA (National Association of Scuba Diving Schools), 24
NAUI (National Association of Underwater Instructors), 24
nausea, 133-34
Nautilus Corporation, 6
neck squeeze. *See* subcutaneous emphysema
nerves, 15-18
neurons, 15-16
nitrogen, 61, 70, 73
nose bleed, 134-35

Oregon plan. *See* Bowerman-Harris program
oxygen, 61-62, 73, 89, 124; bottled, 71, 72, 89
oxygen starvation, 89

padding calluses, 103
papain, 114
Pauling, Linus, 111
physical fitness, 3-7; benefits of, 5-7; new science of, 8-9; tests of, 28-37
physical unfitness, 1-2
platelets, 11
Player, Gary, 41
pleura, 78
potassium permanganate, 92
pressure, 62-65, 120
pressure points, 95, 118
Professional Association of Diving Instructors (PADI), 23, 24, 64, 75, 90; swimming test, 23
pull-ups, 51-52
pulse, taking of, 29-30
push-ups, 51-52

quadriceps, 44, 45-46, 105, 143

recompression, 80
recompression chambers, 69, 74
red corpuscles, 10
red bugs. *See* chiggers
reducing calluses, 102-103
repetitive diving, 82-83

Sargent's Chalk Jump, 34-36
sciatica, 135, 141
scrapes, 86-87
self-treatment, 85-86; basic proce-
      dures, 85-86
Sheehan, George, 96
Shirra, Wally, 2
shock, 101
shoulders, 47-52
Silvia, Charles E., 115, 117
sinuses, 83
sinus squeeze, 83-84
skin, 9-10, 146
skin burns, 86-87
spontaneous pneumothorax. *See*
      lung squeeze
sprains, 135-38; of ankles, 138-39;
      of groin, 140; of hands, 139-40;
      of knee, 140-41; of lower back,
      141; of shoulder, 142; of
      thumb, 139-40; of toe, 142-43;
      of wrist, 144
squeezes, 64, 65
Staubach, Roger, 6
Steinhaus, Arthur, 13, 17
strains, 135-38; of calf, 139; of
      groin, 140; of knee, 140-41; of
      shoulder, 141-42
strep throat, 111
Strykowski, Joe, 3
subcutaneous emphysema, 80
sunburn, 146-48
Sweeney, John, 2
swelling, 148-49
swimmer's ear, 122
swimmer's shoulder, 143
swimming, 22-25
swimming tests, 23

tea, 109
Ten Commandments for Safe
      Diving, 27-28
tendons, 136, 137
tests of fitness, 28-37
      Burpee Thrust, 33-34
      Cooper test, 37
      Goldin one-minute step, 31-32
      heart strength, 30-31
      pull-ups, 34
      recuperative power, 31
      Sargent's Chalk Jump, 34-36
tetanus, 87
thermoclines, 112, 113
Thompson, Acorse, 116
tinea pedis, 90-93
toenails, ingrown, 149-50
toes, 42-44
toe sprain, 142-43
tolnaftate, 91
tourniquets, 95, 118
trachea, 61
Tzimoulis, Paul J., 3

unbandaged wounds, 87
unconsciousness, 150-51
underwater blackouts, 151-52
Underwater Explorers' Society, 24

veins, 12, 20
Vitamin C, 111
*Vitamin C and the Common
      Cold*, 111

Walker, Mort, 75
warts, 152
weight conditioning, 55
weight training, 55
wounds, 153-54
wrist sprain, 144

YMCA, 23, 24, 90

Zonas tape, 96